Praise for *Sixty Meters* ...

"In *Sixty Meters to Anywhere* Brendan Leonard looks
of a misguided youth—had climbing not found him, he would have ...
defined by drink. . . . Inspiration on every page and a remarkable story of determination."
—Conrad Anker, professional climber

"Nothing is off-limits for Leonard in this shocking memoir about
recovery from addiction and redemption in the mountains."
—Grayson Schaffer, senior editor, *Outside*

"Brendan Leonard's prose has the clarity of all those times when, near the top
of a mountain as the air spreads out and the world expands below, you feel as
though the simple, yet mysterious act of ascent could actually change your life."
—Katie Ives, editor-in-chief, *Alpinist*

"Honest as a trad lead, committed as a free solo, this is the story of
how a rope becomes life's gift of redemption—and inspiration."
—Steve Casimiro, editor, *Adventure Journal*

"Leonard's voice is at once crass, funny, heart-wrenching, and life-affirming."
—Chris Kalous, *The Enormocast*

"Leonard switches easily between humor and poignancy,
his voice always unique and yet familiar."
—Fitz Cahall, *The Dirtbag Diaries*

"*Sixty Meters to Anywhere* is an honest, gritty memoir of how climbing and
adventure can help put the pieces of someone's life back together again."
—Stacy Bare, director, *Sierra Club Outdoors*

"There's nowhere as 'exposed' as on a knife-ridge arête thousands of feet above the
earth, connected to a mountain by only multicolored string and some aluminum
knickknacks—except maybe the way Brendan Leonard has exposed how those particular
circumstances changed his perspective forever, and could possibly change yours."
—Jeremy Collins, author of *Drawn: The Art of Ascent*

"Since climbing's earliest days, nonclimbers have asked 'Why?' In *Sixty Meters
to Anywhere*, Brendan Leonard gives the best answer I've ever heard."
—Shannon Davis, former editor, *Climbing*

"In an age where 'adventure' becomes ever more professional and branded,
Brendan Leonard keeps it real. . . . His stories are funny, honest, and
emotional and capture perfectly why adventure feels so important."
—Alastair Humphreys, a National Geographic Adventurer of the Year

"Don't read this book unless you enjoy laughing, adventure,
honesty, humility, and excellent storytelling."
—Peter Brown Hoffmeister, author of *Graphic the Valley* and *The End of Boys*

SIXTY METERS to ANYWHERE

brendan leonard

creator of semi-rad.com

MOUNTAINEERS
BOOKS

Mountaineers Books is the publishing division of
The Mountaineers, an organization founded in 1906
and dedicated to the exploration, preservation, and
enjoyment of outdoor and wilderness areas.

MOUNTAINEERS
BOOKS

1001 SW Klickitat Way, Suite 201, Seattle, WA 98134
800.553.4453, www.mountaineersbooks.org

Printed in the United States of America
Distributed in the United Kingdom by Cordee, www.cordee.co.uk

19 18 17 16   1 2 3 4 5

Copyeditor: Elizabeth Johnson
Design and layout: Kate Basart/Union Pageworks

Cover photograph: *The author on top of Devils Tower* (photo by Forest Woodward)

Library of Congress Cataloging-in-Publication Data
Names: Leonard, Brendan.
Title: *Sixty meters to anywhere* / Brendan Leonard.
Description: Seattle, WA : Mountaineers Books, [2016]
Identifiers: LCCN 2015044406| ISBN 9781680510409 (paperback : alk. paper) |
    ISBN 9781680510430 (ebook)
Subjects: LCSH: Leonard, Brendan. | Mountaineers—United States—Biography. |
    Alcoholics—Rehabilitation—United States.
Classification: LCC GV199.92.L46 A3 2016 | DDC 796.522092--dc23
LC record available at http://lccn.loc.gov/2015044406

Mountaineers Books titles may be purchased for corporate, educational, or other
promotional sales, and our authors are available for a wide range of events. For
information on special discounts or booking an author, contact our customer service at
800-553-4453 or mbooks@mountaineersbooks.org.

♻ Printed on recycled paper

ISBN (paperback): 978-1-68051-040-9
ISBN (ebook): 978-1-68051-043-0

For Mom & Dad

CONTENTS

AUTHOR'S NOTE

This book is a memoir. It reflects my very personal memories of various times, places, people, and events from my past. I have tried to be faithful to the facts and to fairly represent all that I remember, and I have sought input from friends and family. But memory is fallible, and I apologize for any representation that others might recall differently. Some names, places, and other characteristics have been changed to protect the privacy of certain individuals.

LOSER

MY YOUTH ENDED UNDER THE fluorescent lights of a jail cell as my body quivered with dry sobs of shame.

I suppose people mark the end of youth in different ways, if at all: the first day of basic training, college commencement, the birth of your first child, the first day of your first "real job." For me, it was DUI arrest number two: the end of Getting Away With It. It was then that I began to try to be a good person and make up for all the bad stuff I had done but hadn't been caught for—things my parents had raised me to know were wrong but I did anyway. I knew full well how I'd gotten to this spot but I lay there on the bunk trying to find some better explanation.

The cops busted me before our night even got started. One minute I was peeing my name in the snow, and the next I was in the back of a squad car, staring out the windshield, knowing I'd fucked up bad. Again.

Bode and I had finished a few pitchers after our shift at the bar, then stopped to see my pal Jayson, another bartender. He served me the last beer I'd ever drink.

Two twenty-three-ounce Budweisers, one for me, one for Bode. We made half-formed evening plans across the bar, Jayson half-listening to us, half-concentrating on the drink orders piling up from customers, every few minutes mouthing off to us when he stepped across the bar to hand drinks to a waiting server. Cozy golden bar lights, bubbly pilsner getting warm in the tall glass but not faster than I can drink it, big gulps, stubbing cigarettes out in the ashtray, put some bills down on the bar even though the check never comes when your friend is bartending, okay, see you later.

Back in the car, Bode fishtailed around corners through six inches of fast-falling snow, back to his house for a sweater. I waited in the car, parked on the street, engine on.

"Let's go, Bode," I said. *Honk, honk.* "Come on, man." I put the gear-shift in drive, let the car roll forward a few feet, *whoa, better jump over to the driver's seat and hit the brake*, and put it back in park. Red and blue flashers lit up the street, bouncing off the snow. My heart jumped into my throat, then dropped into my stomach.

"Do you have a license?" a cop yelled through the open window.

"I don't, sir," I said. I was fucked. By then, I already knew how hand-cuffs fit. Real tight.

The cops had followed Bode's swerving tracks all the way to the house and found me moving the car a couple of feet down the curb as he stood on the porch. Bode ran through the snowy yard and tried to explain the situation to the unsympathetic officers as I stared out the windshield and decided that if I believed in God, he hated me.

They took me to the police station so we could all have a good time watching me fail at walking heel-to-toe in a straight line. I blew a .12 into the Breathalyzer and immediately demanded they give me a blood test.

We drove to the hospital, and three of them watched a nurse suck a fat finger of blood out of the crook of my elbow while I tried to look tough. I wished they would just shoot me so I wouldn't have to face my mom and dad.

I was almost a year out of college. I was supposed to be an accountant or an advertising salesman or something, not a screwup, a two-time loser. They pushed me back into the puke-, piss-, and blood-proof plastic seat in the back of the squad car, wrists cuffed tight like a real live violent criminal. I had all night in jail to think about what to say to my parents the next day.

I shivered on a concrete bed in a holding cell, looking at a diamond-wire-glass window with my name and birthdate scrawled on it in dry-erase marker—*Brendan Patrick Leonard, 01/16/79*—just above *$3,000*, the amount of my bond. I got a lump in my throat thinking about my dad looking at a seven-pound, six-ounce Brendan Patrick Leonard through a similar window in a hospital in Le Mars, Iowa, wondering if I'd become a doctor or a lawyer or a professional baseball player when I grew up. I wanted to dig a hole in the earth and hide in it until nobody remembered me anymore.

⸺

The next day, after a series of phone calls, I sat watching an indestructible TV with a couple of guys who had robbed someone the night before. My friend Dave was able to bail me out at noon with $300 that he knew I couldn't pay him back. I spent the rest of the day and night in my bedroom, smoking cigarettes and sitting out a blizzard. I mustered the courage to call my mom in the afternoon, and she wailed with disappointment. My heart broke when I told her, just like I knew it would.

She said, "You've got to get some help," and she was right. If I got arrested for drunk driving one more time, I was headed to prison, not jail.

⸺

Later that weekend, after a depressing lunch, Dad and I stood outside my apartment, the snow from the blizzard still blanketing our world.

"Well," he said. "We better get you to Montana."

I'd been accepted to the University of Montana's graduate journalism program the year before, but had deferred my enrollment. Dad loved the West and probably thought it would be a good idea to get me away from all my drinking buddies in Iowa.

I tried to say, "Yeah," but it came out as a sob. I gave him a hug, fighting back tears. I stared at a spot on the ground, trying to swallow a giant knot. There wasn't anything he could do to make it better.

⸻

More than a decade later, my uncle Danny told me that he and Dad had been talking about parenting, in regards to one of my cousins and some trouble he'd been having in school, or maybe his marriage. Danny said that Dad, mostly quiet for the whole conversation, had suddenly interjected, "Well, sometimes you gotta let 'em make their own mistakes."

My dad never hovered over my brother and me, never overreached or made decisions for us, never pushed us too hard in any direction. He was next to me when I landed on my head in my first big bicycle crash, and he took me to the emergency room. He was there when I launched off too-big ski jumps too fast, scattering gear everywhere as I slammed into the snow. He was at every basketball game, watching me turn the ball over too many times, and at every baseball game when a grounder went between my legs. And he listened to all my stories when I was a young, dumb teenager who thought I knew everything.

As a kid, all I ever wanted was some good stories to tell people, some adventures. As an adult, my first real adventures were in bars: How many could we go to in one night, or one day? How many hours could we drink before we passed out? How many shots could we buy the new guy before he fell out of his chair? What about that nightclub across town, or the VFW fifteen miles down the road, or both? When we were done drinking, how fast could we make our car go, and how much stuff could we hit with it? And how many girls could we talk to, and how dumb could we act, and how close could we get to real trouble before we went home for the night? I did all those things and told the stories over and over at the next party the next weekend or on the next barstool.

For a while, it went okay, and I imagine my dad didn't worry too much. I was out there making my own mistakes. But this last one, which made Mom cry, making me cry, I think that might have stung Dad a little more than all the rest of them.

Besides taking it a little too far in high school and spending more time in detention than kids on the honor roll usually did, I was a solid student 3.89 GPA, 31 ACT score could run a pretty quick hundred-meter dash, had good friends, and got along with most people pretty well. But even if you're fine with letting your kids make their own mistakes, I'd guess you still want to do anything to keep them from turning their whole life into one giant sad mistake.

⸺

I wrote the professors at the University of Montana, and Dad put some plane tickets to Missoula for the two of us on his credit card. Our campus visit would be our first big adventure to the mountains since a decade earlier, for a ski trip in Colorado. It was the nuclear option, sending his youngest son thirteen hundred miles away in the hopes it would fix him. With that trip, though neither of us knew it at the time, he opened the door for real adventures, for far bigger dreams than I could cook up over pitchers of beer in Iowa. But before I left, I had to go to court-ordered rehab.

⸺

In the office at the Horizons Family-Centered Recovery Program, I told Mark, the counselor, that I'd already gone three months without a drink. Since my arrest, I'd waited for an open slot in the program. Mark looked a bit like those old portraits of Jesus, but with a trimmed beard and clean hair. He was a patient listener, always making sure I'd finished before he responded.

I figured as long as I always had a pack of cigarettes and a pot of coffee nearby and never had to leave the house except to go to work, I'd be just fine. I was still bartending, albeit mostly during the lunch shift, when only one or two people per day actually ordered a drink. Plus, I could go without the hassle of hitching a twenty-minute ride to the medical center four nights a week and having to restructure my work schedule around it. *Hey, boss, I have to get someone to take over my regular Thursday night shift because I have to go to rehab.*

"You won't make it long white-knuckling it," Mark said. "Not on your own. A person who gets two drunk-driving arrests in one year—blowing more than twice the legal limit at one—is not the type of person the state lets off without sending them to treatment. You need to work the program. The twelve steps have been proven to be successful. You can go ahead and keep your job at the bar, though."

"The program," I said, "is three hours a night, four nights a week, for five weeks?"

"Five weeks is the minimum," Mark said. "You can't white-knuckle it."

Had I been smarter and trying to talk Mark into please, please, please letting me into the treatment center instead of trying to convince him I didn't need any help at all, I would have shared as many of the following items as he had time to listen to:

- I got drunk for the first time when I was fifteen years old.

- My mother's father was an alcoholic. My father's father may have been, but I don't know because he died of tuberculosis when my father was eight.

- When I went out, as many nights as I could, I'd have between twelve and twenty-five drinks. I rarely left bars until closing time, except when thrown out for falling off my stool.

- Lately, I had taken to leaving the bar about a half hour before it closed to buy a bottle of red wine, which I would drink at my kitchen table, while listening to Irish drinking songs and smoking cigarettes. Sometimes I'd start crying and end up sleeping on the kitchen floor until my roommate woke me up so he could make breakfast in the morning.

- I had been in four one-car accidents in the past two years while driving drunk, not counting all the shit I had driven my car into on purpose.

- I drove drunk all the time, and usually kept drinking while I drove.

- I had blacked out dozens of times.

- I had woken up in the morning with women who were not my girlfriend, Amy, women I didn't recognize. Amy and I were often on the rocks, so I didn't beat myself up.

- I was uncomfortable in most social situations, unless it was acceptable for me to be drinking.

- If Mark had asked me about the last time I felt happy, I would have told him about the last time I went drinking with my good friends.

But I was not smarter, and I did not feel grateful to the state of Iowa for opening my eyes to the possibilities of substance abuse treatment. In fact, I felt quite cheated. I was twenty-three years old, and I had to give up drinking for a year. If I violated my probation, I would get six months in jail. Granted, I would find it a lot easier to not give in to the temptation of booze there.

Some of my friends were growing up and not drinking on weeknights, but they still had more than a few beers after work on Friday. The state had told me that I had to quit, that I couldn't legally go on doing my favorite thing in the world. That didn't seem fair. I had been legally drinking for only twenty-five months. What did they expect me to do with my time? Needlepoint? Golf? Go to church?

Still, I didn't have any other options, so I decided I'd quit for one year. It wasn't worth the risk. After a year, I could do whatever I wanted. Maybe I'd even have a new outlook on drinking and I'd be able to keep it under control a little bit more—maybe go out and have three or four beers instead of fifteen. If not, who cares? All I had to do then was stay out of the driver's seat and I wouldn't be in any trouble. I didn't tell anyone else that my no-drinking plan was temporary, but I was already looking forward to being welcomed back to my favorite bars in one year.

⸺

Amy and I were in another hazily defined stage of our on-again, off-again relationship. I'd first noticed her in my information systems class my junior year at the University of Northern Iowa in Cedar Falls. She was pretty, with short blonde hair, and she always wore black or gray. A few weeks later, I offered to buy her a drink in a bar, the first time I'd done that for a girl, hoping to go on a date or two. We became a couple a few weeks before I turned twenty-one, when my drinking turned the corner from fun to disastrous. We drank together, sometimes just the two of us, sometimes with my friends. Some nights she babysat us after we'd already had enough to drink to handicap ourselves—the kind of thing you do when you think you're invincible.

She moved to Omaha just before my senior year, and we took turns driving the four hours to see each other on weekends. If it was my turn, I usually picked up a twelve-pack of some Budweiser at the QuikTrip off the Merle Hay exit on I-80 to get me through the last two hours of the trip, arriving at her apartment with six empty cans in the backseat and hoping she'd drive us to the bar.

In the early years of our relationship, I wasn't good to her. Sober, I opened doors, listened, and tried to be the kind of guy a girl would want to be with. But drunk and a couple hundred miles away, I didn't often act like a guy with a girlfriend.

The day after my first DUI arrest, I showed up in Omaha feeling terrible. I didn't know how I'd ever have enough money to pay for a lawyer, much less the fines. But Amy and I went out drinking. She told me she'd pay for our bar tab, and I drank eleven White Russians, spending money I knew she didn't have. Another time, I called her from a bar back in Cedar Falls and told her I thought I would drive to see her that night even though I'd already had eight or so drinks. When I arrived, she had a deep cough and was having difficulty breathing, but she insisted she was fine, and we went to sleep. A few days later, she went to the hospital and found out she had aspiration pneumonia from making herself vomit up food. Sometimes I think we were just a couple of fucked-up kids.

For a lot of people, college can seem like a time where everyone's partying and making their own bad decisions. I saw plenty of things that helped me rationalize my behavior. I wasn't that different from the guys who were my neighbors and friends, I thought, and my stories from nights out seemed pretty similar to other people's. Eventually, though, when my problems with drinking started to outpace everyone else's, I had to be honest with myself: when I was drinking, I was self-centered, arrogant, and out-of-control.

Now I have the rest of my life to make up for it. I guess you could call it penance.

RECONSTRUCTION

I STEPPED OFF THE ELEVATOR ON the second floor of the Covenant Medical Center and headed for the reception desk. *Day one. Here we go.* I signed in, and a nurse held up a Breathalyzer.

I passed—my first time ever. I almost smiled. It was the simplest thing, only proving I hadn't been dumb enough to drink a bunch of booze right before my first day of treatment, but it made me feel better than I had in a long, long time.

When everyone arrived, I shuffled into a group therapy room about the size of a guest bedroom, behind three middle-aged guys, an older woman, and a young guy. The introductions, shortened from the typical

Alcoholics Anonymous "Hi, my name is Brendan, and I'm an alcoholic," were: "Wesley, alcoholic." "Susan, alcoholic." "Brad, addict." "Jim, alcoholic." "Robert, alcoholic." Then me: "Brendan, alcoholic." And Mark, the group counselor, also an alcoholic. None of us looked like we'd ever be part of the same social circle outside of that room. Mark made the veteran group members read their homework assignments from the past weekend.

Wesley was a grandfather with a salt-and-pepper ponytail and fifteen-year-old eyeglasses. His wife left him, all alone in his house in the country, so he started drinking. He had never really drunk much before and wasn't from a family of alcoholics, but he was bored. After a few months of sitting at home pounding booze, he got pretty used to it. One day, he was driving into town to stock up and a state trooper pulled him over. Because of his high blood alcohol level and a comment that maybe he ought to just end it all, the state recommended he go through a substance abuse treatment program. Wesley was on Antabuse, a drug that would make him vomit and give him vertigo, among other things, if he were to have a drink.

Susan was probably in her early fifties, and eight months ago her doctor had given her six months to live. She had cirrhosis, thanks to the vodka she drank every day to kill the boredom of her life as a housewife. She had three daughters, a granddaughter, and a shitload of other health problems. She had quit drinking with both feet in the grave.

Brad was twenty years old and had a cocaine problem. He lived with his grandparents. When he started treatment, he began to make his bed every day to signal a fresh start and remember to take it one day at a time. Brad was positive and honest, one of those people who was good right to the core. I felt better about myself if he just asked me how I was doing. I made my bed every morning for the next five years.

Jim was a wiry guy with a mustache and a few hard years showing on his face. He was tan, wore a thin gold chain, and looked fifty-five instead of his actual forty-five. He had graduated from treatment, but he still showed up once a week to sit in on group therapy.

Robert was originally from a poor neighborhood in Chicago and had worked his way into what sounded like a pretty successful life. He was on his second marriage in his early forties and was in a layperson position of leadership in his church. He made it sound like he got drunk in his garage a lot.

I felt like Randle Patrick McMurphy in *One Flew Over the Cuckoo's Nest*, when he met all his goofy new neighbors in the psych ward.

I do not belong here. These people are not my people, but they're all I've got for now.

Mark gave me a notebook to use for my homework. My first assignment: write ten "interferences," or ways I interfered in the lives of other people when I was drinking. This was a nightly assignment. Easy enough. I felt I could probably keep writing out ten interferences a day for the rest of my life and still not be done.

When the evening's treatment session was over, we all stood up in a circle, held hands, and recited the Serenity Prayer: *God grant me the serenity / To accept the things I cannot change; / Courage to change the things I can; / And wisdom to know the difference.*

Mark said that the word "God" didn't have to mean "God." It could just be a "higher power," which was anything we needed it to be. It could be the program itself. But I decided that for the time being I was going to go ahead and believe in God, because cigarettes and coffee didn't seem to be quite enough.

I felt hopeful about treatment as I sat on a bench in front of the building, watching the sun set.

My roommate, Nick, rolled up in his red sedan, and I hopped in the passenger side.

"I don't think it's going to be that bad," I said.

⸺

The next morning, I made my single bed, tucking the flannel sheets neatly under the pillow. I only had a few minutes before I had to walk to my lunch bartending shift. I had burned the Peter Gabriel song "Solsbury

Hill" onto a CD after hearing it in the movie *Vanilla Sky*, and had it turned up loud as I shuffled around my small bedroom picking things up.

The hair on the back of my neck stood up. I figured even if Peter Gabriel hadn't intended the lyrics to be about substance abuse treatment, that's what they would mean to me, especially the part about my heart beating, and going home. By myself in my bedroom, I smiled. For the first time in more than a year, I felt like I had a chance.

As part of treatment, I completed a homework assignment every day like "Finish the sentence: I feel good about being sober because _____" or "Finish the sentence: For recovery, I'm willing to _____." Writing down my interferences, though, was like going to confession. Since I knew I was going to read them aloud in group, I kept them kind of tame. I left out the really bad shit. No one needed to know that I'd cheated on Amy, or that I'd stolen someone's car so I could run over stop signs with it. No one had to know that I broke my dad's heart one summer Sunday when we missed a Cardinals–Twins game because I got drunk the night before and overslept in someone's basement, where I'd passed out the night before.

The important part was that I understood that I was an asshole. And I did. I got it. I knew I was an asshole when I hit bottom, or "rock bottom," which is what addicts call the ultimate fuckup—the one that makes you realize it's time to quit.

⸺

My first Thursday of treatment, I looked at all the unfamiliar faces around the circle of chairs: all the wives, husbands, fathers, and kids who had come for Family Night. All the damaged but hopeful loved ones who had all been fucked over by one of us in some way. They were there to help, if someone could tell them how.

We were required to have a family member attend group therapy with us on at least one Family Night during our five-week treatment, and my mom was the first of my family members to join me. She was a sweet little ball of nervous energy sitting in the chair next to mine, leaning forward like always. I felt 45 percent shame that she had to do something like this and 55 percent gratitude to have her there.

She looked at me and smiled as she introduced herself to the group. I swallowed a lump in my throat. She told them she was proud of me for getting help, even though I knew she was disappointed with me for getting myself there in the first place. When she looked at me, I wanted to be fifteen again. I wanted to start over and never take that first drink. I wanted to never put cigarettes out on myself or get tattoos, or have sex with girls I didn't know. I wanted to be that kid on the math team in middle school, the kid who got selected to be in the talented-and-gifted class. I wanted to be an architect or a law student or a physicist, or whatever all those other talented-and-gifted kids are now, not in substance abuse treatment with cokeheads and meth addicts and drunks.

At the break, we all went outside to smoke cigarettes. That's what addicts do: We rely on the last acceptable drug. This was the first time I had ever smoked in front of my mom, the nurse practitioner. She didn't say anything about it.

⸺

When we went back inside, Mom turned to me and said, "I always liked Sundays, because Grandpa never drank on Sundays."

This was the most detailed information I had ever received about her father's drinking problem. He was only around until I was seven years old, when he died of a heart attack at age fifty-nine. When I was a kid, I had no idea that Grandpa was a drunk. I remembered him as a guy who ribbed me about my *Dukes of Hazzard* obsession and took my brother, Chad, and me down to the Emmetsburg fire station to climb all over the fire trucks, where he let us split a bottle of Bubble Up from the soda machine while he did some stuff in the office. Maybe he was sipping a bottle of whiskey back there while we played—who knows.

I asked Chad about it once. He said that all those times I'd asked Grandpa if I could have a piece of gum, the mint we smelled on Grandpa's breath was probably peppermint schnapps. I have never pressed Grandma or Mom or any of her six brothers and sisters for details about what he was like on the days he did drink, if he'd done something that they all carried with them.

⌐

On Family Night, when Mom met Mark, I thought how similar it was to the time I'd introduced her to my first-grade teacher, Mrs. Moore, at parent-teacher conferences. I showed Mom the closet where we hung our tiny jackets and backpacks every morning, and then my sloppy crayon writing on a worksheet hanging next to twenty-five other kids' work. I thought now about how, in a way, I was still a lost kid. In first grade, I was trying to learn how to tie my shoes and walk all the way to school by myself, and now I was trying to learn how to stop drinking beer, something a lot of kids my age had already figured out.

⌐

Robert, the guy from Chicago, relapsed the weekend between my second and third week of treatment. No one really knew what happened, but he didn't show up for group that Monday. His second wife had probably left him. Even so, I thought he was a chickenshit for relapsing, but I didn't say that to anybody. Then I wondered whether he'd decided to take a couple of weeks to go on a pretty good bender before he gave it another shot, because that was sure as hell what I'd do. No sense half-assing it.

I never got the point of doing anything halfway. I'd always been like that to a certain extent, but after treatment it became the one guiding principle of everything I did—especially when it came to staying dry. Growing up, I never shoveled half the driveway or mowed half the lawn, left a homework assignment undone, or tried to get away with slacking at my job washing dishes at a restaurant. So even if I was in the treatment program only because it was one of the terms of my probation, I was going to finish. It was tough, but not tougher than me. This, I later found, was the same mantra that got me to the top of mountains when I felt too exhausted to take another step.

At night after I got home from treatment, I usually spent some time writing, watching movies, or sitting on the front stoop reading and smoking cigarettes. Friday nights were the real bitch, especially during the summer, when I felt like I should be in a lawn chair or sitting out on some bar's back patio drinking myself into a thick mellow hum. The sun would sink, the music would begin to sound great, and all the girls would look beautiful in their dresses, and everyone would wish the whole year would feel like that. It was all I could do to stay home clutching a cup of coffee and a pack of cigarettes.

⸺

The third Monday night of treatment, I met the new guy, Steve. We'd met before, only once, but we recognized each other immediately. During the Christmas season my senior year of college, I worked at a steak house for about three weeks. One of the managers there was nice to me, and one night when I was working she introduced me to her husband, Steve, who came in to have a beer at the bar.

Steve had checked himself into inpatient treatment Friday night, and they'd kept him basically locked in the treatment center, because that's what "inpatient" meant. Among other things, they looked through your stuff to make sure you didn't bring in any cologne or alcohol-based mouthwash or any pills.

He and his wife had two kids, he told the group, and he drank too much and made an ass out of himself at times. He once did a shot of Bacardi 151 and blew a fireball the length of the bar in the steak house where his wife worked. It wasn't the type of place where people got drunk—or expected fireballs—as they enjoyed some country music and waited to dig into a nice slab of beef.

During a break, Steve told me he had gotten so drunk at his own wedding reception that he was passed out by 9 p.m. His wife didn't party nearly as hard, because she was six months pregnant with their first kid.

I nodded, silently confirming that, yes, he should be in rehab. I didn't know a lot of dads who blew fireballs with 151. Most just played golf.

It felt good to have Steve there, as he was the only other person younger than thirty-five since Brad had graduated.

I kept up my routine: Work a lunch shift at the bar, find a ride across town to Horizons in the afternoon, wait for Nick to pick me up, get up the next morning, and walk to work.

When you're just getting used to calling yourself a "recovering alcoholic," working in a bar is not ideal. Though I worked mainly lunch shifts, on Saturday nights I poured hundreds of beers, popping the tap handles forward, then back, watching each glass fill, not too much foam. It all happened twelve inches from my mouth, the smell of beer constant as I poured fifty gallons, dumped out the leftovers, and washed the glasses. I was the gatekeeper for those people doing my favorite thing, just on the other side of the bar. I didn't have another way to make a living, or I would have quit. Instead, I steeled myself as best I could, and gave my free shift beer to whoever tended bar with me that night.

One Wednesday afternoon, after the lunch rush had died down, a guy walked in the door and sat at the bar. I thought I recognized him. He ordered a gin and tonic, and when he spoke, it clicked. I walked around the bar to pour a one-shot count into a short rocks glass and peered at him over the upturned gin bottle.

"Jim?" I said.

"Yeah?" He seemed unfazed by the fact that I knew his name.

"You recognize me from anywhere?"

"Nope," he said. "Never seen you before."

"Jim, I know you from treatment," I said. "Brendan? Horizons?" *Ring a bell? Jesus.*

"Oh, yeah," he said. "How you doin'?"

"I'm good. Listen, should I be serving you this drink?"

"Oh, yeah," he said. "It's fine. I fell off the wagon last weekend."

"Oh," I said. "All right then."

"Yeah, we found out my wife was pregnant," he said.

What?

I shot the shit with him for a few more minutes, and he ordered another drink. He took off before my shift was over. He didn't even tip me. I didn't tell anyone from treatment about that evening. I figured it wasn't a positive development for anyone.

⸺

In that group therapy room, I experienced true, authentic empathy for the first time. It felt so safe when all the normal walls were knocked down. I could be vulnerable, and in turn care deeply for people I'd only known a few weeks. I didn't want Wesley to kill himself. I wanted DHS to leave Susan's family the hell alone, even if her daughter smoked too much pot. I wanted her to survive cirrhosis so she could take care of her granddaughter, who didn't sound like she would have much of a chance.

By the end of a session, I felt like we had all been through the Normandy Invasion, and I didn't mind hugging people I didn't know at the end of the night. On Family Nights, our group met in a big room with another treatment group the same size as ours. I didn't know those people as well, but I wasn't jaded or cynical. When they spoke, I nodded and gave encouraging smiles. As much as possible, I told them they were doing the right thing.

⸺

One night after treatment, I sat on the front stoop of the house I shared with Nick and Dave, drinking a cup of coffee and lighting up cigarette after cigarette. I was reading *The Old Man and the Sea*, and I realized that reading was about the only healthy addiction I'd ever had.

When I was in third grade, I was obsessed with books. I read all the time. I stayed in to read so often during recess that my teacher told my parents that it might be good for me to go out with the other kids and get some fresh air once in a while. Every time I finished a book, there were others waiting, pulled off my parents' bookshelves or checked out from the library. I read so many pages for the school reading program that the local newspaper published a small story on me. This, as far as I can remember, was the first thing that had completely consumed me. But other things soon replaced it.

⸺

My dad dressed up for his visit on Family Night, changing out of the black pants and white shirt he'd worn every day for a couple of decades behind the meat counter. I figured a room full of junkies and drunks wouldn't have judged him if he wore dirty work clothes, but it was a nice gesture. He nodded and listened as I told him about what we did there, showed him the place, and introduced him to some of the folks from my treatment group. I wondered if he was thinking that this might be the strangest thing we'd ever done together.

Dad had knocked off work early that night, just like he'd knocked off work to be at every single event I had competed in since I was six years old, including the spelling bee in sixth grade. I was never very good at basketball or football or track, but attendance is the love language in my family. On Family Night when he said he was proud of me, I got a lump in my throat and blinked back the tears as Dad talked to a room full of strangers. I resolved to myself that I was not going to suck at sobriety.

Dad heard Terry's daughter talk about her high school graduation party, how Terry wasn't there because he was at a biker bar using meth. She said she was happy he was getting help.

Dad also got to hear Tom's wife tell everyone how they got in a fight the other night. When he stormed out of the house, she said she just knew he was going to a pay phone to call his meth dealer, but he didn't. He just went for a long walk to cool down. She cried as she told the story. Wesley scurried over from our side of the circle to hand her a box of Kleenex.

When it was our turn, Dad told everyone he wished he hadn't let me do what I was doing when he knew I was doing it. Like when he came to pick me up to go out to lunch and saw the tickets tacked to the wall of the house where I lived in college: *Underage Possession of Alcohol* and *Possession of an Open Container of Alcohol*. I remembered how I thought it was funny and we both laughed about it on the way to the restaurant.

I shook my head when he told the group that he could have done something, and I denied that it was his fault in any way. That was the truth.

The truth is, my mother had always warned me of my genetic predisposition to alcoholism. I had the earliest curfew of any of my friends when I was a teenager. I don't know if anybody knows what they're doing when they start raising kids; all they can do is their best. My parents' best was seventy-hour weeks at a grocery and third shift at the hospital, so my brother and I could have a basketball hoop in the driveway and presents under the tree when our mom got home from work at eight on Christmas morning.

I had patches on the holes in my jeans when I was a kid, but not before Mom and Dad had patches on theirs. When I think about my tired mom wearing her nurse's uniform while walking down to the elementary school next to a little kid with snot in his nose and a jar of grasshoppers in his backpack, and I think of my dad staying up all night putting decals on toy fire trucks even though he was beat from smiling and selling Christmas hams for fourteen hours, I know it's not their fault.

When I think of all that, I feel tremendous guilt, and the tears well up in my eyes. I want to put my fist through a window.

⸺

Some time after my stint in treatment my friend Craig's son checked into a Hazelden treatment center to deal with a heroin problem. Craig called me and asked what he could do to help, what he could say to his son. I told him, based on my own battle, I didn't really think there was anything anyone could say—that you have to figure it out on your own.

⸺

One afternoon on my way out the door, I found a card in the mailbox asking me to RSVP to my five-year high school reunion. *Oh, hell no.* What was I going to tell people? Reunions are where you go to talk about your accomplishments. That sounded like a nightmare: explaining to everyone that I had graduated from college, become a bartender, and enrolled in substance abuse treatment. *Oh, but if things work out with my court case, I'm going to move to Montana in the fall to pursue a master's degree.* No, thank you.

The Friday before my fifth, and what I hoped was my final, week of treatment, I sat at the rehearsal dinner before Chris and Kerry's wedding, my first friends from high school to get married. I couldn't drink enough cups of coffee as everyone else ordered another beer and another beer and another beer. I would have given anything not to be there, but Chris had asked me to be an usher, so I showed up. I left the rehearsal dinner before anyone else and I made it early to the church the next day. After the ceremony, the wedding party boarded a bus, and everyone except me started pounding more cans of cheap beer. A few miles down the road, we stopped to visit Chris's mom's grave.

She had contracted some sort of rare illness, degenerated quickly, and died a couple of months before the wedding. I had hitched a ride to her funeral with another high school buddy and three of his friends, who drank all the way to the service and all the way back.

Now after Chris and Kerry's wedding ceremony, we stood there in front of Linda's grave, and Chris's dad, Franny, held up his beer and said, "Here's to ya." Everyone else held up their beers, and I shoved my hands deeper in my tuxedo pants pockets. Standing in front of your friend's mother's grave on his wedding day and not having a beer to hoist in tribute is a bit too much for anyone to be asked to deal with. I left the reception early, hoping Chris and Kerry would understand.

⸺

On Monday afternoon, I tucked into our cozy little group treatment room for my last week of rehab. When it was my turn to talk, Mark asked how the wedding had gone. I told everyone that I had, in fact, controlled myself. As I spoke, it suddenly struck me that there was a possibility they might not believe me. But as I glanced quickly at Wesley and Mark, I was relieved to see that actually, yes, they did. This room full of people who had been strangers now knew my struggle better than anybody in at that wedding reception.

On my final Thursday, my graduation night, I read my last homework assignment, my After-Care Plan. I wondered if I'd ever write another thing in that spiral notebook. After five weeks of picking me up at the front door of the building, Nick came in for Family Night and introduced himself as my brother.

Nick was my best friend, for many reasons. I had met him at the Applebee's restaurant where we worked during college. He was always ready for some fun. We met when we were twenty and found out we shared the same birthplace, Le Mars, and that we had been baptized by the same Catholic priest.

I liked Nick because he would never turn down a couple of beers, he was funny and animated, and he knew a lot of girls. I think they liked him because they could tell he wasn't trying to sleep with them. He was looking for a girlfriend, not a one-night stand. We played off each other's jokes and introduced each other to new people. We even looked a little bit alike. Sometimes people would ask us if we were brothers. He was never in a bad mood and once loaned me $300 so I could pay my rent that month, not knowing if I'd be able to pay it back. I did. And now he gave me rides home from treatment every night. He had earned the privilege of sitting in a circle with a bunch of addicts and alcoholics and their family members.

At the end of Family Night, and my last group session, Wesley gave me a big desperate smile, and we hugged as he planted a wet kiss on my cheek. Sometimes I think about that look. We both knew we'd never see each other again, and his eyes pleaded, *Goddamn it, kid, I hope you do it, because I don't know if I can.*

When Nick and I got home, he went in the house, and I sat on the front stoop, smoking a cigarette that felt like a five-minute exhalation. I still had a weeklong jail sentence to serve before I moved to Montana, but a huge chunk of my sentence was finished.

The next week, I had to attend one after-care meeting, the last time I'd ever see the Covenant Medical Center and the Horizons program. I told Nick I'd get a ride home from someone at the meeting, but really I wanted to walk. It was a chance to remind myself how grateful I was that he had interrupted his life four nights a week for five weeks just to pick me up.

It was nine miles home, and it took me three hours to walk it in the dark, in sandals. That was the end, my certified completion of a court-ordered twelve-step substance abuse treatment program.

They do incredible things for you, all those open, understanding, hopeful faces and voices in the group therapy room. They know you can beat your addiction, some days more than you do. But one day you have to leave that cozy little womb of hugs and Serenity Prayers, and you have to step out the clinic's sliding doors all by yourself. A chapter is over. You wait at the curb for a bus or a friend with a car, and you light a cigarette, and maybe then you realize that no one told you what to do with the rest of your life.

They don't tell you that you'll have to reinvent yourself, which is difficult when all you really know is that you used to love to get fucked-up. That's not much of a starting point when you're making small talk with someone new at a party. *Hi, my name's Brendan, and I don't drink anymore. That's the absolute first thing I want to tell you about myself, because learning how to not drink anymore has pretty much consumed my life for the past year. So, what about you? What are you into?*

I felt like the only examples I saw for life after treatment were people who either found Jesus, became more or less addicted to Alcoholics Anonymous meetings, or relapsed. Recovery is a great time to be "saved" or "reborn" religiously, and being addicted to AA meetings is of course healthier than alcohol.

If you don't stay strong, you relapse, and even if you stay strong, relapsing sounds like heaven—you just shut off that voice in your head by giving it what it wants: buckets of cold beer, whiskey Cokes, gin and tonics, and tequila shots. You resign yourself to being a loser and singing along with "Piano Man" every time it comes on.

If, however, you don't decide on Jesus, AA, or falling off the wagon, you have to find something else. I had no ideas, but I was intent on escaping Iowa. Now five months sober, I had to talk to someone about leaving the state while on probation. I wasn't sure it was possible.

⸺

It was raining in the not-so-great part of Waterloo, where my dad drove me to meet Dave Davis, the man who would be my probation officer. We waited with everyone else in a big room and listened to a guy tell us about random piss tests and how our probation officer could call or stop by at any time to make sure we were home by curfew. If we screwed up in the least, it was a year in county jail.

After the rules guy left, we waited for our individual appointments with our probation officers. I was pessimistic about my chances. I couldn't imagine that Dave Davis would let me leave the county, let alone go to graduate school three states away.

But Dave was a great guy. Once we started talking, it was clear that he didn't have a lot of appointments with people who were pursuing advanced degrees in the liberal arts. Everything was going to be just fine. The system? He'd sign this little piece of paper from the Iowa Department of Corrections, and I could show it to a cop if for some reason he needed to run my ID. All I had to do was send in one hundred dollars of my fine per month, along with the corresponding payment coupon for Dave.

When we walked out of Dave's office, I was sure no one else there was even headed to college. I felt grateful—and guilty. What if Wesley did this same sort of meeting with a probation officer? He'd drive into Waterloo, check in, and then drive back out to his lonely farmhouse. No potentially bright future, no new scenery—just the same situation that led him to drinking in the first place.

CRIMINAL

I BROUGHT A TWO-FOOT-HIGH STACK OF books with me to the Chickasaw County Jail in New Hampton, my hometown, my last obligation before I left Iowa for grad school. For my first stint in jail, in Iowa City, I hadn't brought anything with me, so I'd had to borrow my cellmate's only book, something by Louis L'Amour. I read that book from cover to cover, like any sane man would have if the alternative was staring at the ceiling or out the six-inch-high diamond-wire-glass window on a cold, gray October day.

This time, I made damn sure I had enough books, and I brought *War and Peace* as a backup. If ever there was going to be a point in my life when I had enough time to read a thousand-plus-page chunk of Russian literature, it would be while doing time in the county jail.

Marty, the county sheriff, was kind enough to let me take up a bunk in the jail for seven days near the end of the summer. Even kinder, he let me split my sentence up into two three-and-a-half-day segments so I could attend a drinking driver education class over the weekend. He was sort of familiar with my dad from around town, so we talked a little bit about football and other stuff before getting to the standard intake interview.

"Height?" he asked.

"Five ten," I said.

"Weight?"

"One sixty-five."

"Hair?"

"Brown."

"Eyes?"

"Blue."

"Scars?"

From my past experience, I decided it was easier to just show him. "One here," I said and pointed to the two-inch scar running across my left forearm. I had run into a barbed-wire fence one time when I got drunk my senior year of high school.

"And one here," I said, lifting up my shirt to show him the scar that ran armpit to armpit just under my nipples, another souvenir from the fence.

"Four cigarette burns on my arms—here, here, here, and here." I never remembered how much the previous time had hurt.

"All right. Any tattoos?"

"One here." I patted underneath my right arm. "5-31-97." I had gotten it right next to the armpit-to-armpit scar to remember the date it happened.

"Okay."

"And one on my lower back. 'Too weird to live, too rare to die.'" I looked at the form he was filling out to see if he would misspell "weird." It was one of those words that usually took everyone, including me, a couple of tries.

"Any others?"

"One more on my ass. It says 'A tattoo.'"

"No shit?" He smiled as he wrote it down.

"Yeah. Once upon a time, it was a great party joke."

"I'm sure it was. Have you ever tested positive for the HIV virus?"

"No."

"Use intravenous drugs?"

"Nope."

"Ever have a seizure?"

"Nope."

"Homosexual?"

"Nope."

"Ever tried to kill yourself?"

"Nope."

"Thinkin' about tryin' it while you're in here?"

"Nope."

"Okay. This next part probably isn't your favorite. Strip down, turn around, and face the wall."

Up until this point, I could pretty much rationalize that I wasn't a real criminal; I was just a guy who drove after having a little too much to drink.

"Show me the bottoms of your feet . . . Bend over and spread your cheeks . . . All right, stand up and turn around . . . Arms over your head . . . Okay, arms down. Lift up your scrotum . . . Okay, get dressed."

When an officer looks in your ass for drugs, though, the line between you and the "real criminals" is suddenly a lot blurrier. I followed the sheriff down a steel hallway. I had always wondered what was in this building when I drove by it in high school, never really expecting to find out.

"We'll put you down here by yourself until we need this cell," he said. He carried my books, and I carried my rubber mattress and pillow, sheets, blanket, towel, soap, toothbrush, comb, deodorant, and plastic water cup.

Down the corridor we went. I wanted to knock on one of the walls, but my hands were full. There must have been a bolt driven into them every three inches along the seams. I wondered if the same people who built ships also built jails.

My cell door double-locked, tight enough to keep out a rush of water should the jail go under in a tsunami. Inside was a shower, sink, toilet, television, and two bunks. Steel bars on one side, steel walls on the others. Even the toilet was made of steel, with a push-button flush and no seat. You had to sit on the rim of the toilet, which most folks only do in the middle of the night when someone else has forgotten to put the lid down. You could wash your hands only one at a time, as your other hand held down the sink button that made the water run.

The bunks had one-inch holes to provide a little air under the body-fluid-proof mattress. The holes would also ensure that any cellmate on the upper bunk who pissed his bed also pissed on the lower bunk, and me.

I threw my collection of jail-issue stuff on the bottom bunk and turned on the TV. Antenna broken off, no knobs, just a safe plastic ten-key cable box to change the channels. I walked back across the cell to my bunk. Three steps.

Above the toilet, there was a video camera, which would give whoever was on the other end of the closed circuit a full-frontal shot every time I urinated.

I moved my books from the bed to the floor, flipped through the television channels, and settled in. The mattress was lumpy and hard, and the pillow was little more than a waterproof bag of loose stuffing. It was like being quarantined in my college dorm room for a week straight, but with even crappier food and no interaction. I wanted to tell the sheriff I had changed my mind about doing my sentence just then.

I had the whole first day to myself. They fed me through a slot in the door at exactly noon and again at exactly 5 p.m. I watched TV until I got bored, when I picked up a random book and read with the TV sounding in the background. Time moves very slowly when you can't stop thinking about the next three days.

I slept surprisingly well for a guy who'd spent the entire day lying in bed. Until midnight, anyway, when I got two roommates. They were both intoxicated and loud, but I couldn't hold it against them. Anything is loud in a room made of steel. One of the guys jumped up to the top bunk, and the other dropped his mattress onto the floor. I pretended to be asleep, because I didn't know what to say. *Hi, I'm Brendan. I'm actually serving a seven-day sentence right now. How about you guys? DUI, I assume?* Eventually, they stopped talking, and I fell back asleep.

Three days passed, and at the end, my brother, Chad, came and got me. We had arranged it so my mother didn't have to drop me off or pick me up from jail. My dad and my brother took care of it. Chad brought me a pack of Camel Lights, and I lit one as soon as I got in the car. We went to McDonald's, then home, where I got to do the things I had been fantasizing about for three days: use a clean toilet —seat intact—eat non-jail food, and take a private shower.

My mother and I left that afternoon for Cedar Rapids, where I attended drinking driver education school for the second time. The content of the class was the exact same as the one I had taken the previous summer—twelve hours of information about how many people are killed each year by drunk drivers just like me and the twenty other people in the room. I had obviously not learned anything my first time around.

⸺

Saturday night, we drove back home. At 10 p.m. Dad dropped me off at the jail to finish the last three days of my sentence.

This time, I got my own cell for the first night. The next morning, they moved me in with the rest of the guys in the eight-man cell. Everyone glanced up when I walked in, then went back to watching TV.

Nobody introduced themselves, but I picked up enough about them from their conversations and our brief exchanges.

Paul was two months away from release, serving six months for possession of crystal meth. He had a few missing teeth and a black mullet. Paul liked to talk about anything, but mostly what was on TV at the time.

Todd was a few days away from finishing a four-month sentence for something he never mentioned. He had a blond mullet and didn't talk except to affirm anything Paul had said.

Jeremiah and Abe were awaiting trial on burglary charges. They had been caught breaking into a car-wash office the previous weekend and had so many priors that they were looking at a minimum of five years in the state penitentiary. They spent a lot of time fantasizing about cigarettes, hatching plans to have one of their mothers bring them a smoke on the day of their trial. Maybe they'd have time to suck it down during the hundred-yard walk from the jail across the street to the courthouse. I couldn't believe that was all they were worried about. I also couldn't wait to have a cigarette, but I didn't have to consider a looming prison sentence. They were going to do a large amount of time in a very bad place because they jacked about a hundred bucks worth of quarters from a car wash.

Jimmy was sweating out a few more weeks until his trial for five counts of statutory rape. He didn't look like he was more than eighteen or nineteen years old, and I felt sorry for him. If no one else noticed the irony when Jimmy said, "Jesus, she's hot," about a seventeen-year-old Avril Lavigne on TV, I did.

Out of the six of us, I got dealt the best hand. Hell, two weeks after I got out of jail, I'd be in Montana, going to graduate school. Jimmy, Jeremiah, and Abe could all be behind bars for at least a few years. Todd was getting out in a few days, but not to a very posh life. You don't get a lot of great job offers after you've done four months in the county jail, especially in a county that small. Same for Paul. I hoped I'd be applying for jobs where my prospective employer didn't do a criminal background check on me, and if they did, they'd let me explain my situation. But that was way off in the future.

I didn't fit in. Well, I fit in because I was a criminal like the rest of them and we were all wearing the same jumpsuits, but I wasn't going back to the same life everyone else was. I didn't say much about myself at all, other than that I was there because of a second DUI and that I'd graduated from New Hampton High School in 1997 (go, Chickasaws). I definitely didn't mention grad school. I felt a little guilty about my secret, but more so I just wished the time would pass faster. I wanted to somehow fall asleep for seventy-two hours and wake up when my brother showed up again.

It was hard to keep my attention on the words in my books when there were five other people talking in the small room, plus a TV. I'd read for a while, then try to sleep. Of course, when there's nothing to do but sleep, you can't sleep.

I sighed, I itched, I changed positions on the bed, then repeated. I looked forward to my trips to the toilet, because they broke up the monotony. I forced myself to drink water so I could get out of my bunk and pee more often.

I looked at the clock and counted the hours until my release, working the numbers over and over in my head, trying to make them seem shorter by breaking them up differently. *Okay, it's two in the afternoon, and I get out at eight on Wednesday morning. It's Sunday. That's two days and eighteen hours. Or sixty-six hours. Sixty-six hours. I'll be sleeping three more nights here, so maybe eight hours a night. If I'm lucky, that's twenty-four hours of sleep. So, really, I only have forty-two more hours of awake time. That's 2,520 minutes. Sixty seconds in a minute times 2,520 minutes—what is that? Like 150,000 seconds. If I try to count to 150,000, by the time I'm done they'll be calling my name to tell me I can go home. Or, I could count to 50,000 every day. That might work better. One . . . two . . . three . . .*

I usually counted to about eighty before losing concentration.

The other guys would go outside in the yard every afternoon, but I stayed in. I didn't want anyone in my hometown to see me in a jumpsuit, playing basketball at the county jail. It was a small town, but as far as I knew, no one I went to high school with had learned I was a big failure. I wanted to keep it that way.

—

War and Peace plus Jimmy, Paul, Todd, Jeremiah, and Abe was an exercise in futility.

> And it was indeed only for a few steps that he ran alone. One soldier started after him, then another, until the whole battalion with a shout of 'Hurrah' had dashed forward and overtaken him. A sergeant of the battalion darted up and grasped the standard which was swaying from its weight in

Prince Andrei's hands, but he was immediately shot down. Prince Andrei snatched up—

"Look at this fucking lady."
"What?"
"This lady on *Springer*. Check out them shoes."
"Oh, yeah. Those are fucked-up."

Prince Andrei snatched up the standard again and dragging it along by the staff ran up with the battalion.

I wonder what time it is.

In front he saw our artillerymen, some of whom were fighting, while others had deserted their guns and were running towards him.

Maybe it's 2:30. I should look at the clock. No, I shouldn't. The longer I read without looking at the clock, the better.

He also saw French infantry pouncing on the artillery horses and reversing the field-pieces. Prince Andrei and the battalion were now within twenty paces of the cannon.

It's probably 2:30 by now. It sounds like that TV show is almost over. I don't even need to look at the clock. I'll just listen for the closing and opening music of these shows and I'll be able to guess by that.

He heard the incessant whizz of bullets overhead, and to right and left of him soldiers continually groaned and dropped. But he did not look at them: he kept his eyes fixed on what was going on in front of him—on the battery.

2:21. Shit. That's why I shouldn't look at the clock. I'm too optimistic about how fast time is passing. I'm not going to look at the clock again until I read fifty more pages . . . Okay, maybe twenty-five more pages.

That's how it went, for three days.

⸺

On day two, everyone else went outside to the yard, and it was just me and a guy who had just arrived. I didn't know his name.

I nodded and said, "How ya doing?"

"I gotta talk to my lawyer," he said. "I can't do this."

Really? What the fuck do you mean you "can't do this"? This whole system is built around making you do this. You can't just call your mom to pick you up because you're not having fun, or sneak out in the middle of the night and end up with a dishonorable discharge. You have to do it. It sucks. That's why they send you here when you do something bad.

There is no feeling in the world like having your freedom taken away, for a few days or months or years. I will never forget it.

⸺

I woke up early on my last day. I didn't sleep much the night before. Once the clock said 5 a.m., I got up and packed up my mattress and pillow. My brother would be there to pick me up at eight.

Breakfast came at seven, and I let Paul eat mine. He said thanks, and I think it was the first time I had looked him in the eye. I tried to watch TV but ended up checking the clock every minute.

At eight, nothing happened. Obviously, the guards weren't as excited about my departure as I was. Finally, after four minutes that felt like forty, the door opened. The guard carried my books, and I squeezed out the door with the rest of my stuff. No one looked up from the TV to say good-bye, but in my head, I wished them all luck.

BIG SKY

WHEN I WAS A CURLY-HEADED five-year-old trying to hit a T-ball in our back-yard, I'm sure my mom never looked out the window and imagined that one day she'd be dropping me off in Montana, just a month out of sub-stance abuse treatment and a week in jail. I suppose I also would have cried there on the steps of the apartment in Missoula, if I were her.

I had no money, no car, no driver's license, and no friends. Amy and I had broken up. She had supported me, long-distance from Omaha, through rehab, but without a license, I was unable to visit her much, and we'd seen less of each other after my last arrest. I was twenty-three. I was skinny, depressed, and alone. I was about to check off my sixth month of sobriety, which suddenly felt like six days. I had no idea what was going to happen to me in Montana, but I tried to act calm for my mom and dad. It was a long way from the humid ballfields of southwest Iowa, where tan, stubby-legged kids kicked up dirt and tried to care about winning.

I wanted my parents to go, sort of, so I could smoke a cigarette and figure out how this whole Montana thing was going to work. They needed to get back, anyway, and there wasn't much to say. Something like *Son, as long as you don't fall off the wagon or hang yourself, we'll be fine* would have covered it.

So we stood there, Mom, pursing her lips, on the verge of tears, and Dad, still taking in the view to the south: the grassy slopes of Mount Sentinel and the buildings of the University of Montana at its base.

"You'll call?" Mom said, hugging me one more time.

"Of course." I didn't have much else to do in that apartment on Front Street in the week before the start of classes.

Missoula was beautiful. With two rivers and Rattlesnake Creek cutting through town, and pine-studded mountains on three sides, it was the idyllic West. My father had briefly lived out west, then left to go back to Iowa for a secure job when he was about my age. He wasn't worried—he'd have been happy for me if I had been starting a job on an assembly line if it were in a place like Missoula.

Me, I didn't know. It seemed far enough away from my recent past that I could start over, but it wasn't like they didn't sell beer in Missoula. They sold beer everywhere in America. All I had to do was not drink any of America's beer every single day for the rest of my life.

As my parents turned their car out of the parking lot, I imagined my mom sitting up straight as a board in the driver's seat, hands at ten and two, crying but trying to smile.

I was scared. I felt as alone as I did on my first day of preschool, when my mom left me in a room where I didn't know anyone. I was the kid who cried the whole first day. I turned toward Mount Sentinel and lit a cigarette.

My new apartment still smelled like someone else's that whole first week in Missoula. I walked around downtown a bit during the day and spoke with my mother almost every night, not knowing what else to do with myself.

Missoula was like no other town I'd ever been in—people walked everywhere with their dogs off-leash, and when dogs weren't allowed into a shop or a bar, they waited contently outside, sitting on the sidewalk. Higgins Avenue was home to three coffee shops, and none of them was a Starbucks. At Taco del Sol, you could get a gigantic veggie burrito for under four bucks. (The first time I ate there, I had to be told not to take the foil off all at once—you left it on and peeled it off as you went, so that the burrito kept its shape and contents.) Two outdoor gear shops sat within four blocks of each other. Bicyclists rode on the street right next to the cars, unlike in Iowa, where no one rode a bicycle anywhere unless they'd gotten a DUI and lost their license. (After my DUI arrests, I purposely walked to work, even though it was slower.) Everyone had beards or long hair or dreadlocks and fleeces or ski jackets, or cowboy hats and Carhartts. The cars all had roof racks for skis and bikes and kayaks, and license plates from every US state. Maybe I could grow a beard.

⸺

I shrank more each time a new person introduced themselves to Professor Dennis Swibold's class in room 201 of the journalism building on my first day of fall semester: Hans, originally from Sweden, had a master's degree in Holocaust studies and had interned as a photographer at the *Telegram & Gazette* in Worcester, Massachusetts. Nic was a vegan from San Francisco who said he'd been inspired by the work of Henri Cartier-Bresson; I assumed Henri Cartier-Bresson was a photographer. Andrea was originally from the East Coast, had a master's in public administration, and hosted a show on the UM campus radio station. Gwen was a member of the Salish and Kootenai tribes, and she had worked for Sony and Al Gore's presidential campaign. Linsey was originally from Bigfork, Montana, and had an English degree from the University of Portland. Kristine had worked extensively in public relations and marketing for radio stations in Oregon and Texas. Tim, originally from the Washington, DC, area, had a degree in zoology from the University of Maryland, and had hiked all 2,190 miles of the Appalachian Trail in one six-month stint.

Hi, I'm Small-Town Guy Who's Never Been Anywhere. I barely graduated from Public University in the Great Plains, and I just got out of jail. What the hell was I doing in the same room with these people? I was from a town with six stoplights, had traveled to exotic locations such as Des Moines and Omaha, and spent parts of my summer in a cell and a group therapy room. *Oh, and I wrote a little bit for my college newspaper. In my spare time, I like to chain-smoke and fight a constant compulsion to drink alcohol.*

A couple of weeks into the first semester, when we were in the hallway outside our editing class, Hans suggested going out for beers.

"Yeah," Tim said. "We should."

I tried to mention that I didn't drink anymore without making it sound too strange. It sounded really strange.

"That's okay," they said. "You don't have to drink."

I know I don't have to drink, jackass. I understand that they don't pour beer down your throat the second you walk into a bar. I know they won't kick you out of most establishments for ordering a water.

"Well, I'm on probation," I said, "and my probation officer says I can't even go into a bar, so I'll have to hang out with you guys some other time."

The first time they went out for beers, I was probably sitting at my apartment, clicking away on my computer, popping out the front door every hour or so to smoke a cigarette.

It had been a little less than six months since what I now hoped was my last beer ever, and a little more than eight years since my first one: a can of Miller Genuine Draft Light I'd stolen from my parents. It was May or June of my freshman year in high school. A bunch of us were at a friend's house in the country.

I sipped the beer and tried to look like I knew what I was doing. There were a few older kids, and most of the kids my age had already been drunk a time or two. It was raining off and on, and we sat out on the patio, talking and listening to somebody's Creedence Clearwater Revival cassette. The beer was so bitter I could barely swallow it. I couldn't finish it before the summer air warmed it up. I wanted to at least develop a taste for beer so I could hang out with my friends without feeling like a weenie.

My friends and I had already had conversations about whether or not we were going to drink in high school, and a few times I'd mentioned that my father had offered me $1,000 if I didn't drink until I turned twenty-one. He didn't have the money, but I think he either guessed I wouldn't do it or hoped to scrape it together by then.

My friends said that was okay, that I could be the driver.

In my high school, I think 90 percent of alcohol was consumed in cars slowly driving around the hundreds of miles of gravel road that crosshatched the county. We didn't need a "designated driver"—you could drive those roads from 7:30 p.m. to midnight and not see another car—but my friends wanted to make me feel better about my uncool choice. I didn't last long not drinking, though.

A few weeks after I had my first two-thirds of a Miller Genuine Draft Light, on the Fourth of July, I managed to get drunk off of Old Milwaukee and some stale Black Velvet whiskey pilfered from my friend Scott's grandmother's basement fridge. Her house was right across the street from Saint Mary's Catholic Church, where I spent every Sunday morning and church holiday for four and a half years. Poor Agnes never had any idea what we were doing. She died when I was in college.

I don't know how I mustered up the courage to drink enough beer to get drunk, but I remember how incredibly excited I was by the warmth, the slight dizziness, and the slowing of my senses.

My curfew was 10 p.m., so I stayed over at a friend's house as often as possible. A bunch of girls in our class were having a sleepover a few blocks away, so we made sure to stop by and show them how drunk we'd managed to get. I mean, after you've had your first six or eight beers, you're pretty much an expert, even if you drank them all at once.

I think they were pretty impressed, although I never came out and asked them. I hardly had hair in my armpits, and I was drunk.

About six months passed before my peers started ribbing me about my ridiculously low tolerance to alcohol, and another six months passed before I got my driver's license. That Soundgarden song "Black Hole Sun" was the theme song to my first summer of drinking, playing every other hour on every radio station we could pick up in rural Iowa. For the first time ever, I had something that felt like confidence. It was empowering, though it should have terrified me to know it only came from a twelve-pack of beer or a bottle of liquor.

⸻

I rarely look people in the eye when I'm talking to them. My eyes dart around, looking at the ceiling, the floor, the table, the window, and only once in a while, the other person. I'd like to think this is because my brain moves too fast, that I can't stop to stare at someone's face.

I've met guys who are very straightforward, who always look you in the eye and smile. I've always wanted to be just like them in that respect—I'd like people to feel like they can trust me. But I can only handle a second, maybe two, of direct eye contact.

Similarly, ever since I was a kid, I haven't known what to do with my hands in a public place. If I was in a park, at a baseball game, in a shopping mall, or crossing the street in front of a line of cars, I was worried people could tell I was uncomfortable.

In fact, ever since I was old enough to recognize confidence in other people, like the kids who played quarterback in our third-grade touch football games out on the playground, I've been trying to look like I know what to do with my hands. I used to suck them up into my coat sleeves, but I quit that when I realized I was old enough that I needed to start acting like a man. Pants pockets were usually good but couldn't be relied on too much. I bit my fingernails until I was in ninth grade, when I got braces and couldn't squeeze my fingertips in between the metal. And then I started going through puberty.

For two consecutive high school football seasons, my face exploded into what's clinically known as "severe nodular acne." Red bumps the size of BBs or a little bigger appeared on my cheeks, chin, nose, and neck at the rate of two or three per day. Health professionals tell you not to pop or pick at zits and pimples, and I tried, but most days I couldn't stand to go to school with three or six pus-filled whiteheads sticking out of my face like spikes on a blowfish. I'd rub a bath towel across them after I got out of the shower, and the heads would rip off and bleed. I thought at least they looked a little flatter after that.

My mother took me to a dermatologist shortly after I got my first pimples, my freshman year in high school. I took antibiotics to prevent acne for a couple of years and had the typical teenage pimples until my junior and senior football seasons. My face was a minefield of clogged pores—more red than flesh-colored, and bumpier than Mars. My face *hurt*. I wished I could skip school, but, hell, it wasn't like the zits were going to go away the next day, so I went to school. I hated it when I had to talk to girls and they'd look me in the eye. I knew they were thinking I had never seen a bar of soap or had some horrible infection on my face, and I'd look away.

When it was the worst, the dermatologist recommended Accutane, a drug that could cause such serious birth defects that women who took it had to be on two forms of birth control. It dried out the skin on my face so badly that I had to smear Vaseline on my cheeks and forehead every night before I went to bed, and sleep with an old towel over my pillow so I didn't ruin it. I suffered night blindness the second time I took Accutane, during my senior football season.

The dermatologist also gave me an oral steroid, prednisone, to take some of the inflammation out of the nodules in my face. After a while, he didn't want to prescribe it anymore, so when I went in for my checkups, he'd inject cortisone into some of my zits with a small syringe. When a doctor sticks a hypodermic needle directly into your face and you're not even worried if it will leave a mark, you don't wonder if your acne is abnormal.

My friend Dan asked me in the locker room once why I had so many zits.

"I think it's because of my football helmet," I said.

He said he wore a helmet too, and he didn't have any. "Do you wash your face?" he asked.

"Yeah," I said. "I don't know why my face looks like this. I guess God hates me, Dan."

One time I was working at the concession stand during a girls' basketball game, and a ten-year-old kid asked me what was wrong with my face. I didn't know what to tell him. I hoped his zits would be twice as bad as mine when he was seventeen. Or that he would get his nose bitten off by a Rottweiler.

It hurt my mom that my face was so ugly, I think. She pitied me. I was sad because girls didn't like me. I didn't have a date to the homecoming dance my senior year.

A few years later, I found out that Accutane caused depression, and in a few cases, suicide. And of course, you're not supposed to drink on Accutane, which I knew the entire time I was taking it. How was I supposed to not drink? I was seventeen, girls didn't like me, I had a face that looked like a pepperoni pizza, and all this happened during the dark, dead Iowa winter, arguably pretty depressing even when you're not taking little yellow pills that make you want to kill yourself.

I got drunk whenever I could get a night off from my dishwashing job and could score beer. I learned how to drive drunk along the gravel roads at thirty-five miles per hour, with a couple of friends in the car, listening to Pearl Jam cassettes and stopping to pee in ditches as the freezing wind screamed across the dormant cornfields. Sometimes we'd clip cans of warm beer under the windshield wipers to cool them down as we drove. Maybe we weren't the most popular guys in school, but we were friends, and I wasn't lonely.

During my first semester at the University of Montana, I got back to my empty apartment early on Fridays, with nothing to do. Sometimes I'd stop at the store in the University Center and pick up a thirty-two-ounce fountain soda to last me through six or eight cigarettes. I always felt like I should stay on campus and study, but on Fridays, no one was around, and I couldn't make myself stay somewhere as deserted as the university library.

On Friday afternoons, the hikers and campers and mountain bikers and their dogs were on their way out of town on I-90, Highway 93, or Highway 200. The partiers were back at home smoking a bowl or drinking a few beers, and others were at happy hour at the downtown bars. Whatever anyone was doing, they were doing with other people. I was headed home by myself.

Back at my apartment, I would lie on the floor with my head between my stereo speakers and try to nap for about twenty minutes, or I'd check my email, or I'd start downloading another album. Every hour, I'd smoke a cigarette on the second-floor balcony outside my front door, and I'd put it out in my "ashtray," an empty four-pound Jif peanut butter container with old coffee grounds in the bottom. It filled up monthly. I wished it didn't.

Around seven, activity would pick up around the apartment complex. Loud music started to play and people carrying six-packs or twelve-packs came and went, some in cars and some on foot, since downtown was only four blocks away. Besides the music coming out of my stereo, my apartment stayed quiet.

Every hour, another cigarette. Sometimes the people walking by saw me up on the balcony. It was awkward. I felt like I had to say hi to the people below. They were dressed in their going-out clothes, and the girls always looked great. I remembered a time when I used to be able to talk to college girls like that. I tried to act like I was looking at something else when they passed me, but I knew they could tell I was avoiding them.

Not so long ago, after I'd gotten through the bad-acne stage, I was them: good-looking, lightly buzzed, telling jokes, confident, smiling, laughing. But now I was a sad, nervous loner who wished I could just smoke inside his goddamn apartment instead of having to go outside, where the entire world could see me.

At least early in the evening, no one was drunk enough to talk shit to me. But even if they weren't trying to be mean, people yelling an intoxicated "Hey, man. How's it going?" or "What's up, man?" made me wish I was invisible. I could only muster a feeble, sober "Hey, man," back, the first hoarse words I'd spoken to anyone in seven hours. I was like the freshman geek trying to reply to the hottest senior girl in school the first and only time she asked me how I was. It never came out right.

Saturdays, I'd wake up late and call friends back in Iowa. I never had much to report. I did my laundry. I killed a few hours by walking over to campus to work on an assignment in the computer lab or at the library, where I figured maybe an attractive girl might spontaneously start talking to me. A long shot, but my chances were better there than inside my apartment. Or I could go downtown and get a cup of coffee at the Raven Cafe. They had two tables for smokers out on the sidewalk. If one of them wasn't open, I'd usually just keep walking. Unfairly, I didn't like one of the girls who worked there, because I sometimes heard her talking about trips to South America. She represented everyone in Missoula who was more worldly than me, which was pretty much everyone.

Sooner or later, the sun would go down and I could go back and hide in my apartment. I felt lonely when I went out at night, bumping into all the guys who could drink or had enough money to go to the movies or take girls out to dinner. The people who had friends. So instead, I'd smoke cigarettes and wish I were invisible, watching old movies on my VCR. If I was lucky, my classmate Tim would come over and smoke some of my cigarettes and watch a movie or two with me.

Sundays, I woke up late again. I'd walk the three-quarters of a mile to the grocery store, wearing my empty backpack, with a mental list of things I'd like to buy. I could fill up only one basket, because if I went over that, there was no way I could carry everything home. A full basket would mean a couple, if not three, plastic sacks from Albertsons on each hand, squeezing all the blood out of my fingers and knocking against my knees as I walked. Besides, I always got a sick feeling in the pit of my stomach as the cashier rang it up, wondering if I'd have enough money to make it to the end of the month.

In the afternoon, I'd call my parents. In Missoula, calling my mom felt good, because I was being honest with her for the first time in a long time. Some Sundays, my parents were the only people I'd talked to since I left class on Friday.

—

I wonder if everyone has a period in their life when they're at least a little lost about what it is they're supposed to do. You tread water until the boat marked *New Identity* comes by to pick you up. Sometimes it takes years. You're never in danger of drowning; you're just listless, maybe frustrated enough to feel like screaming *How fucking long do I have to do this?* For me, it was when I lived at the apartment in Missoula.

Eight years after I'd left Montana for good, after I'd climbed all over the West and started to get some momentum in my writing career, I laughed at how well thirty-two-year-old me would have fit in as a grad student at UM, and how out of place I was when I'd lived there.

Weekends in Iowa during my senior year in college had gone more like this: On Friday afternoons, I'd get out of class early and begin nursing my hangover from Thursday night with a couple of Bloody Marys at the Other Place, one of my favorite bars. Or I'd grab a few beers with my neighbors across the street—or anyone else who happened to be around and thirsty. Some days, I'd meet a friend at two for a late lunch at the OP, and we wouldn't leave until eleven thirty p.m. or so. I'd always be too drunk to remember to pay my tab, and I'd have to go back on Saturday and have them run my credit card for the $120 I could barely cover. Some Saturday mornings, if I didn't have to work, I'd sit down, pay my tab from the night before, and start drinking again.

I'd drink all afternoon and return home at five or six to shower before I went out that night. I felt more alive than I ever had in my entire life. Anything could happen—I could get in a fight, get arrested, go home with a girl, or all three—hopefully in a strip club. The more crazy elements, the better the story the next day.

During college, I felt finally accepted. Because I was a regular, I always knew at least ten people, who would introduce me to ten more.

Sometimes girls recognized my face from the column I wrote for the campus paper, the *Northern Iowan*. I was on a first-name basis with many of the bartenders, so I rarely had to wait long for drinks. I also tipped like I could actually afford my habit. If my friends and I couldn't get in, I'd slip the guy at the door a twenty.

We hoped to meet girls, we lit things on fire, we bought drinks for people we didn't know, we did shots with the bartenders, we took over parties, and we got thrown out of bars, but we looked good doing it and everyone loved us. I belonged somewhere for the first time ever. Or that's what it felt like.

Who knows how it really was. By midnight most nights, I was so intoxicated that I would stumble around with a glass of whiskey in one hand and a lit cigarette in the other, accidentally burning people and mumbling, seeing the world out of my one half-open eye. No college student should be able to rack up a hundred-dollar bar tab in a place that sells domestic beers for a dollar seventy-five. But I did, frequently. And sometimes, at the end of it, women I wasn't in love with would take me home.

⸺

Remembering those times made me feel even worse when I stood outside my apartment in Missoula two years later, with no friends, no good-looking women, and no whiskey to drown my sorrows, even by myself. I hated Missoula, but just because I hated myself.

Loneliness made me want to drink, to go inside bars and find a seat and somebody—hell, anybody—to talk to. But everything made me want to drink. Including but not limited to: being by myself, oldies music, being around other people who were drinking, being around other people who were drunk, lawn furniture, sunsets, being anywhere in Iowa or the Midwest or just driving past a cornfield or a soybean field, Saint Patrick's Day, Saint Patrick's Day parades, New Year's Eve, my birthday, the ten minutes every day after I got off my work-study job at the business school, the smell of fresh-cut grass or a barbecue, looking in the front window of a bar as I walked past, the smell of cigarettes and/or fried food, the Doobie Brothers, Creedence Clearwater Revival, any Southern rock album, Bob Marley's *Live!* album, the smell of dust off a gravel road, dashboard lights, the smell of beer, the smell of stale spilled beer in a bar, seeing college-age kids dressed up to go out, eating dinner at any restaurant that served alcohol, wedding receptions, work Christmas parties, bonfires or campfires, golf courses, and the sound of the crowd at a college football or professional baseball game on television. And other people asking me if I want to go have a drink with them.

When meeting someone for the first time, an alcoholic must make it clear that he or she will not be joining that person and/or anyone else for drinks, beers, or happy hour. This can be accomplished by politely declining the very first invitation and explaining that he/she is a recovering alcoholic. At least that was my strategy. I don't know if anyone ever wanted an explanation, but I always felt like I had to give them one. On my 173rd sober day, I walked the seven blocks to the basement of the First Baptist Church in Missoula, where about twenty people sat and drank the watery coffee that they serve at AA meetings. This was my second AA meeting ever; the first had been required for me to graduate from treatment. I thought this one might help, since I was having a hard time meeting people.

I wanted so badly for it to be good for me, like rehab had been. I wanted to walk out the door and smile when I was sure no one was looking and get a little lump in my throat because I was proud of myself. But it wasn't like that.

Most of the people there were kids who had been ordered to go to AA by some juvenile court. They sat in the back and picked at their fingernails, waiting for someone to sign the form for their probation officer. The real alcoholics opened up their hearts and lives to each other and desperately tried to find the answer that would make them okay again.

I didn't speak up at the meeting, since it was my first. When it was over, the organizer asked everyone who was new to the group to come up to the front. She handed me a flyer with a list of the eighty-three other AA meetings in the area and with five handwritten phone numbers next to the names of people listed under the heading *My New Friends*. I told her next Saturday was my six-month mark, and she excitedly said I should come back so I could get my six-month chip. I said I would.

I walked up the steps, back onto the sidewalk, and down Pine Street, and hurried across Higgins Avenue, where all the normal people in the world were enjoying themselves at Stockman's, The Top Hat, Feruqi's, The Rhino, Sean Kelly's, and a dozen other places within six blocks of each other. All those people had friends and laughs and good times and good conversations, and all I had was a cigarette on the way home.

‗

I didn't want to go back to the AA meeting the next Saturday. It didn't make me feel much like being a recovering alcoholic, and my first meeting in Missoula would be the last AA meeting I ever went to. There was probably a better one somewhere else in town, or a better weekend to go to the one at First Baptist, but I just never went back. I started to find something else instead.

My cousin Alissa, who had recently graduated from UM with a creative writing degree and was still figuring out what to do next, invited me to go backpacking. Almost completely ignorant of backpacking, I said yes, and on a Saturday afternoon a couple weeks later, jumped in her car for the drive to Glacier National Park.

Eight hours later, I could feel the seam joining the wall of the tent to the floor along my back and legs. We had pitched it on the ground next to the Granite Park Chalet, which was closed for the season. I was grateful that Alissa had invited me to go to Glacier with her boyfriend, Whitney, and another friend, Allison, but as the fourth person squeezing into a three-person tent, I felt a little like maybe I shouldn't have come along. I hadn't slept all night; I just kept wishing I could close my eyes once, then open them to find it was morning. There was no moving without pushing everyone else around. If this was what camping was like, I was pretty sure I didn't like it.

Alissa had rented the tent from a gear shop in Missoula, but I think if they saw what we were doing to it, they'd probably halt rentals. I couldn't believe the sidewalls of the tent could handle the pressure we put on it. From the outside, it must have looked like a nylon sack holding together a pile of people at the bottom.

As soon as I could see light through the roof of the tent, I unzipped my borrowed sleeping bag and shimmied my way out the tent door. I put on my shoes and walked away, into a dizzying 270-degree panorama of mountains with glacier-cut stripes sweeping horizontally across their faces. This is what I hadn't seen as we'd hiked up to the chalet in the dark the night before.

I had tried to be helpful, even though I didn't know how to light a campfire or set up a tent, I didn't have a proper backpack, a flashlight, a Swiss Army knife, or a compass. I had no idea what to do if I got lost, saw a grizzly bear, or had to take a crap. I had just followed everyone up the switchbacks north of Going-to-the-Sun Road and tried to act like I knew something about what I was doing.

I waited for everyone else to get up and out of the tent as the sun gradually warmed me enough to take off a couple of layers. After breakfast, we hiked northeast over Swiftcurrent Pass, and at the crest, the horizon fell away into a three-thousand-foot green gorge with three lakes along the bottom. I set my foot on a rock and stared. It was like a painting. My heart pounded.

After a few minutes and a few photos, we turned to go back the way we came. Then I lit a cigarette on the trail in one of America's most beautiful and flammable national parks. Everyone looked at me like I had just pissed in the punch bowl at a wedding—especially Allison.

"How long have you been chain-smoking?" she asked.

I was embarrassed. "Three and a half years," I said. "It makes not drinking a little easier." I thought about putting out the cigarette and admitting that I was an idiot. But I told them to go ahead and I'd catch up, as if that would reassure them that I wouldn't light the largest forest fire in the history of Glacier. I had no idea what I would do if I did spark a fire. It wasn't like I had a fire extinguisher in my backpack. I held my cigarette really close to the trail, hoping the wind wouldn't blow an ember onto a pile of dried pine needles and make me the biggest asshole in Montana.

I caught up with them a few minutes later, and after a quick snack of stale Corn Nuts, Allison and Whitney filled their water bottles directly from a stream coming down the mountain. They said they were immune to giardia. I did not want giardia. I did not fill my bottle.

Then there was a mountain goat, and everyone got excited. I tried to act cool, as if I walked to school with mountain goats every day back in Iowa.

We started up some switchbacks that led to a lookout building at the top of a small peak. It was warm as I plodded up the all-rock trail, one step at a time. I peeled off my jacket, then my sweatshirt. Up and up, my stomach rumbled and my feet hurt. Finally, I reached the top, a few minutes behind everyone else.

The building was a weather observation station, tied to the top of the rocky ridge with tension cables. The wind whipped around us. It was cold again. *Are we on top of a mountain?* I thought, but I didn't ask anyone. If we were, it was the first mountain I'd ever climbed.

Whitney pulled a prescription bottle from his pocket and pulled out a joint out. He smoked most of it and gave Alissa a puff. I figured it was okay to light a cigarette now. I made Alissa take my picture, twice. I smiled big, but only on the inside.

Could I come back here? What does it take to be a person who does this stuff every weekend? Can I be in the mountains again, and breathe the air, and feel small?

⸺

The next Friday, I stood on the front porch of my apartment on Front Street in another cold cloud of cigarette smoke and self-doubt. As usual, I watched all the other students come and go, wondering how I'd gotten so old in less than a year.

Who says I have to get this sobriety thing right the first time? Lots of people get second, third, and fourth chances, especially celebrities. They treat rehab like it's junior high detention. Look at Robert Downey Jr., for God's sake. What's the big deal? You fall off the wagon; you go back and get some more treatment.

They keep this up for years, back and forth. Why can't I do that? I mean, the pull is there, the gravity. Who could blame me? The people who really care just say shit like, "Oh, it's so hard for him," when you screw up. And when you go back to rehab again, they say, "He's really trying."

I tried—and didn't fail—my whole first semester at UM. I was miserable, but I didn't fail. I barely made my student loan money last the whole semester, budgeting just enough for cheap cigarettes. Nicotine gave me a tenuous grip on sobriety. I lost weight and looked skinny, maybe unhealthy. I booked a flight back to Iowa just before Christmas, a couple of days after my last class.

My final night in Missoula, I spent the last of my cash on a delivery pizza, large, and ate the whole thing by myself. The next morning, I got on my first flight of the day and immediately felt a fever coming on. Free of the stress of that first semester, my body relaxed into a crushing head cold.

⌐

Back in Iowa, I slept late and snuck out of the house to smoke cigarettes in the front yard. And I started to notice something different about my mom.

Every night of my life before she went to bed, my mother would take a bath and put on her pajamas. She would nestle herself next to the arm of the couch, feet curled up underneath her, with her rosary and a single can of Bud Light. Just one beer, as she silently said the rosary and watched the weather forecast for northeast Iowa. Every night, just her, Jesus, and the weatherman, having a beer and some Hail Marys.

She'd nod off about ten times before she'd finally go upstairs to bed. I never saw her drink more than one beer at a sitting—except once at a wedding. I think she had two, but I can't be sure, because I was on number eight or nine by then.

Then when I became a certified fuckup alcoholic, she quit that routine. I noticed one night when I was in the basement doing some laundry. There was no beer in the mini fridge, the one they used for Diet Coke and bottled water because the well water was brown. But I saw a couple of twelve-packs shoved in a back corner beneath a table, under some old towels she used to dry the dog off after a bath.

"Oh, yeah," my dad said. "She hides the beer when you come home."

"No shit?" I asked.

"Yeah, I don't know." He shook his head and chuckled.

"Jesus," I said. "Does she think I'm going to freak out and start pouring it all down my throat?"

"I don't know," he said again, shrugging.

"I'm twenty-three years old, Dad. I can go buy a case of beer if I really want to drink."

⸺

Back in Missoula that spring, I spent late evenings sitting on the filthy couches in the crumbling newspaper office in the basement of the J-school, correcting punctuation, grammar, and spelling, and smoking cigarettes with a couple of the other late-night staffers. On Thursday nights, we got to watch three or four Renaissance Club kids in full armor beat the shit out of each other with fake swords.

One Thursday at about midnight, I walked home from the newspaper office under a full moon. The whole city had been dusted with snow. I crossed the Madison Street Bridge, and for once the icy Hellgate Canyon wind didn't try to rip my jacket and face off. I glanced up to see Mount Sentinel and Mount Jumbo lit up, their snowy peaks reflecting the light of the moon. I stopped and let out a breath. I had not been more tired, depressed, or lonely in a long time. There was no going back to my life in Iowa, but I wanted to be in those mountains. I wanted to follow the backpackers and mountain bikers and kayakers and skiers, rambling among the ghosts of old miners and loggers and Salish and Kootenai Indians.

SORRY

AFTER ANOTHER COLD WALK TO the grocery store, I stood in the soda aisle, gauging whether the taste of a twelve-pack of soda was worth the pain of carrying it the three-quarters of a mile home. Ten minutes later, I was struggling down Front Street with about eighteen pounds of liquid—the soda plus a gallon of milk.

I had four plastic sacks on one hand, and two more, plus the gallon of milk, on the other. As I got closer to my apartment building, I could see four guys walking through the parking lot, crossing right in front of me. They were probably headed downtown for a night out. I hoped they'd just ignore me, but as I got closer, two of them looked up. I said, in an assertive but friendly tone, "What's up, guys?"

A couple of them nodded, and their friend asked if I needed some help.

"No, that's cool, man. I got it," I said, knowing that drunk college guys didn't have much of a reputation for helping other guys carry their groceries.

"No, man. I'll help you," he said. "I can carry your bleach."

"It's actually milk," I said. "That's okay, really. I got it. I'm just right here." I pointed up to my apartment, literally about ten steps away.

"No, man, come on. Let me help," he said, reaching for the milk.

Rather than have him tear it out of my hands, I held it out for him, knowing full well what would happen. He took it, and I stepped onto the first stair.

I heard my gallon of milk explode on the asphalt, then laughter, then footsteps running off.

I unlocked my door and carried the rest of my groceries inside, wishing I had a gun. Instead I grabbed my pack of cigarettes and a hammer and went back outside, my heart pounding and my jaw clenched. I hoped the guy would come back to the building and cross in front of my door. I rehearsed in my head the best way to hurt him without killing him. Arm, leg, balls.

If that asshole knew how much it took me to get a gallon of milk home. I don't have any friends, or a car, or money. I'm almost a year sober. He has no idea what that's like.

I neared the end of my cigarette and slowly realized that if that asshole knew half the things I had done while drinking, he wouldn't feel the slightest bit bad about smashing my milk. If the world was at all fair, I'd had that one coming a long time.

A few weeks before college graduation, I came home drunk and sprayed my roommate with a fire extinguisher as he slept. He was the third person I'd sprayed with a fire extinguisher. I set our couch on fire a few weeks later, on purpose. I spent hours trying to talk a girl into having sex with me one night when all she wanted to do was sleep. I used up ninety-six eggs on my friend's car one twelve-degree night—they froze—when he refused to drive to the casino with me at 2 a.m. In high school, I spray-painted the f-word on a few farmers' propane tanks out on gravel roads. I probably hacked off their mailboxes, too. I ran my truck into the cable that held up the light pole for my high school's baseball field, causing about $1,000 in damages. During my first DUI arrest, I insinuated that I'd had sex with the arresting officer's wife, among other things that eventually led him to slam me into a wall inside the police station. Once, I hit a car in a McDonald's parking lot and then left. I drove my truck through many people's yards, mostly going after their trash cans. I stole someone's car and joyrode it over several stop signs before parking it in someone else's front yard, wiping my fingerprints off everything inside, and running off. I figured out, with the help of a guy who owned an auto body shop, how to get $1,600 from my car insurance company. Then I spent the money on booze and left my car the way it was after I'd driven it off the icy road and into the ditch on the way to the casino. I reported my mountain bike stolen, making $1,200 in insurance money for booze, and found out later that it really was stolen. I threw up on a booth and myself during the dinner rush at a family pizza place. I called my best friend a loser to his face for no reason. I stole five or six cases of beer from the restaurant I worked at in high school. And that's only what I can list in five minutes.

Over time, I started to understand why bad things happened to me. They say your luck gets worse and worse as you keep drinking. Lots of people believe in different religious or spiritual systems of good and evil, where you're repaid for bad things either during your life, during an afterlife, or during reincarnation. I didn't have a name for it; I just recognized that when I was bad to people, whether I meant it or not, whether I was sober or drunk, bad things happened. The universe found a way to kick my ass. And sometimes it was a literal ass-kicking.

⸺

The first time I ever got the shit beaten out of me, I don't really believe I deserved it. I was a sophomore in college and had just moved to a new apartment. It was three blocks from campus and two blocks from my favorite bar, where everyone figured I was twenty-one. This particular night, I was just about to leave the bar when a waitress asked me if I wanted some free shots. She had been trying to sell these dollar shots of schnapps in test tubes all night, and she had a few left over after the bar closed. I shot about eight of them in a row while trying to talk her into going home with me. When she kindly declined, I said good night and walked out into the street.

Some sort of race riot seemed to be going on. Black guys and white guys were pounding on each other all over the street. A few weeks earlier, some sort of rumble had happened at a club across the street between the rugby team and some gang members from Waterloo, and this may have been a continuation of that.

I saw this white guy named Tyson getting shoved around by five or six black guys in the middle of the street. I had met Tyson through a coworker, and we chatted occasionally, but we never got much closer than that. I should have just walked down a block and over to my house, but instead I walked straight into the chaos.

All I remember after that is a black guy punching me in the face. The next thing I knew, some huge white frat guy was dragging me off the street into Tony's, the club where everything had apparently started, and asking the bouncer for some ice. I had pissed my pants, I guess, or maybe I had fallen into a puddle, and blood had spattered all over my shirt.

James was the frat guy's name. He said his dad was an anesthesiologist or something, and he knew a broken nose when he saw one. He was going to take me to the hospital. I would rather not go to the hospital, I told him, but he wouldn't listen. He said a bunch of black dudes had been kicking the shit out of me. I told him I supposed it didn't really matter if they were black or white. My lip was swelling up. I made him stop at my house and get a disposable camera.

At the hospital, I asked the nurse to take my photo, for my own personal evidence. There were a couple other bloody white guys there, and a cop, who asked me a few questions about who had beat me up, none of which I could answer. "Some black guys," I said. "That's all I know." *Does that help? I'm sure you'll have them tracked down in an hour or so, sir.* I had no idea who they were, and I didn't care. I just wanted to go to bed.

The nurse started messing around with my nose in the X-ray room, and when I lay down on the table, facedown, I left a pool of blood the size of a dinner plate.

I couldn't really sleep that night. I called my dad at work at six in the morning and told him what happened. He asked me what I was doing in the middle of something like that, and I tried to downplay it with a joke.

My mother took it less well, worrying about brain damage. I thought it was kind of funny. I thought it made me tough. But that was really early on in my drinking career. I didn't deserve it in the way I deserved it a couple of years later, after I had stacked up some real bad karma.

⸻

One of those times was in Ottumwa. It was the violent and necessary end of my third and final RAGBRAI trip, the Register's Annual Great Bike Ride Across Iowa, seven days and 475 miles that took us from the Missouri River to the Mississippi River. The ride passes through about fifty different small Iowa towns every year and brings about twenty thousand cyclists with it. Some are serious, but some are like my team, the Bloody Choads, who drank our way across the state, treating RAGBRAI as our own spring break, only in the middle of the summer.

My night in Ottumwa had been going okay. I'd been able to convince a septuagenarian farmer in the last town, Albia, to drive me thirty minutes there after I'd been drinking all day. He threw my bike in the trunk of his car and drove me to my destination, where I promptly bought him the three beers I had promised him at some dive on the west end of town.

A few hours later, I met up with my teammates at the American Legion, where they had set up camp, and we went to a bar packed with people. I bought some guy a shot of tequila, and he paid me back with three more in the next ten minutes. It was enough to just about send me to the floor.

I left the bar a few minutes later, staggering all over the downtown sidewalks and totally unable to find the parking lot of the American

Legion. I had not been that drunk and still standing in years—maybe ever. I got drunk three or four days a week, I blacked out, I threw up, but I almost never staggered. My body was shutting down.

I stopped at a pickup truck where some younger folks were drinking and asked for directions, and one guy stepped forward and said that since I was one of those bike riders, I needed my ass kicked. I said that no, I didn't, that I'd like to just find where the American Legion was.

The guy punched me in the forehead, and I reeled backward a little, just in time for the second punch directly on my cheekbone, same side. *This is not good*, I (slowly) thought, and I turned to run. I stumbled maybe thirty or forty feet before he kicked my legs out from underneath me and I fell to the pavement, face-first.

I awoke alone, no pickup truck forty feet away, no people nearby. I could hear the creek running downhill from me, and when I realized I had shit my pants, I thought about diving in to rinse myself off. My ribs and face hurt. I got up and started walking.

I accosted the first couple I saw and told them Ottumwa was the biggest shithole I'd ever been in. I had blood all over my face and bare chest, which may have been what caught their attention. I told them what had happened, and they gave me a ride to their house in the back of their truck. There was room in the cab, but I think they could smell me. They gave me a can of beer and a clean towel, and through the bathroom wall, I could hear the woman calling someone and telling them what I'd said about my one-sided fight. She was outraged that something like that could happen in her town. I was too.

When they gave me a ride back to camp, I found my teammates drinking with an older couple named Bear and Mary. Bear told me that he used to get in all sorts of trouble when he stayed out late. Once he quit staying out late, he quit getting in trouble. He was giving me advice, but I was too stupid to understand. I thought he meant I should just drink at home from now on.

When I got back from the trip, feeling mistreated and wanting to blame someone, I wrote a letter to the *Des Moines Register* about my experience. The *Register* printed my angry, naive letter, blaming the town of Ottumwa, and a reporter called me to follow up with a story. She pointed out that I had never reported the incident to the police, had never registered for the bike ride (we hadn't in three years of riding), and had been drinking (which I'd admitted over the phone). So I got beat up, but I was the one who ended up looking like an asshole.

A few nights before Ottumwa, three girls I'd never seen before picked me up in Ankeny and took me to Ames, where one of the girls and I messed around in someone's bedroom, and then I never talked to her again. Amy and I were not officially "dating" that summer. I think we had talked and decided that we should "take a break," or I used some other wording that made me feel okay about wanting to hit on other girls.

So I deserved what I got. When you treat people like dirt, sometimes other people will treat you like a punching bag. Sometimes this happens just days apart. A couple of years later, I stopped believing in bad luck.

⸺

On my 365th day of sobriety, at Altered Skin on Brooks Street in Missoula, I watched a buzzing tattoo needle rip into my skin, just above my left bicep. Watching the needle seemed to make the pain less sharp—I could see it coming.

I had decided I needed a tattoo instead of an AA chip for my one-year, so on the exact day, I walked down to the shop and showed the artist a piece of paper with some ideas. I spent a hundred dollars of the little money I had and got two tattoos: a claddagh wrapping around my left arm just under my shoulder, and a crown and a copyright symbol on my right shoulder, a sort of signature of the '80s pop artist Jean-Michel Basquiat. He was a hero of mine who had died of a heroin overdose long before I'd ever heard of him.

I walked the mile home in the cold spring air, over the Higgins Avenue Bridge, with fresh blood and fresh ink on both arms, prouder than hell of myself for making it through the hardest year of my life.

⸺

A month later, everyone else in Missoula was partying and I was out front smoking another cigarette on my second-floor porch. I had warmed up a cup of coffee in the microwave and was sipping it with my cigarette. Three guys I recognized as my neighbors walked across the parking lot to their Honda Accord. As the two guys standing by the passenger side waited for the driver to unlock the doors, they both looked up at me.

"Just havin' a cup of coffee and a cigarette," one said, just loud enough for me to hear. Then they got in the car and drove away.

Anger welled in my chest and bubbled toward the top of my head. They had lived there long enough to know my Saturday night routine. To them, I was a lonely old lady in a housecoat and curlers, a sad fixture on my porch watching all the neighbors live their young, exciting lives. I hated them for having the freedom to go out on the town and talk to girls and drink a little too much. I hated myself for not having anything else to do, or knowing what to do. You could have wrung the desperation out of me and filled up a bathtub with it. I had no social life and no friends. Well, one friend.

⟺

Tim and I had started the journalism program together. He was built like a runner, slight but strong, some of that probably due to his thru-hike of the Appalachian Trail two summers before he came to Montana. He was from Silver Spring, Maryland, and had majored in zoology during his undergrad because it had "sounded interesting." He smiled big and laughed loud, and was always happy to take a smoke break with me. Unlike me, Tim had a bit more of a social life, but he found time to hang out with me once in a while on the weekends.

At the end of the first semester, Tim left the journalism program, because he wasn't getting what he wanted out of it. I hadn't considered what I wanted out of it; I had arrived in town to get a master's degree in journalism. I had never thought further than that. After he quit journalism school, Tim stayed in Missoula, working remotely for a software company and thinking about going to law school, but we didn't see each other in class on campus anymore, just at the Raven for coffee or a weekend hike. Tim could talk movies and books and music and life almost nonstop, and seemed like he'd already explored every trail within an hour of Missoula in our short time there.

⸻

One late spring Saturday afternoon, Tim and I started hiking up the back side of Mount Sentinel. It was my first time going up that route, but I trusted Tim to know what to do if it got dark on us before we finished.

After a mile or so, we met up with the Hellgate Canyon Trail, which climbed sixteen hundred feet through the evergreens and some unmelted snow to a jeep trail named Crazy Canyon Road. It was nearly pitch-dark when we hit Crazy Canyon Road, which took us a steep quarter mile up to the top, almost all by moonlight.

At the top was a view of Missoula's lights, stretching out onto the plain. Tim said the view was actually better from farther down the front side, closer to the giant white concrete M that hung about six hundred feet up from campus. The lights of the city bounced around as we started down the trail, closer to jogging than walking.

A few hundred feet down, we sat without talking, watching a plane slowly cover the six miles over the valley from the Bitterroot Range to land at the Missoula Airport at the far northwest end of town. We had to be the only people on that mountain just then.

⸻

Near the end of my second semester in grad school, the clouds lifted off Missoula and the sun came back for good, not going down until almost 9 p.m. Everyone under the age of thirty switched to dresses and tank tops and shorts, throwing Frisbees around campus, riding skateboards and bikes, and taking their time outside instead of rushing between heated buildings. It was once again the sunny Missoula you see on all the college brochures.

A few weeks before the end of classes, I planned to skip the Dean Stone awards banquet for the School of Journalism, despite the fact that it was taking place two and a half blocks from my apartment, at the Holiday Inn. Everyone gave me shit about it, until I finally went to Professor Swibold to explain that I was skipping the banquet because, well, I was a recovering alcoholic, and I really didn't know how to handle myself yet at functions where everyone had a few drinks—no offense. He said he understood.

As I stood on my porch smoking another cigarette, drinking some coffee, and wishing I knew how to act around large groups of people again, they announced my name for the A. B. Guthrie Memorial Scholarship, and Professor Swibold had to go to the microphone to tell everyone that I couldn't be there that night.

⸺

One afternoon, my dad called as I ate lunch in my dim kitchen. He said he'd gotten pulled over the other night.

"For what?" I asked him.

"Well, you know, I had to drive down to the Waverly store to get some filets, because we were out and we don't have a truck coming for another week. So I drove down, and you remember my friend Kent?"

"Yeah, kind of," I said.

"Well, he sold that Bourbon Street bar in Cedar Falls and opened up another bar in Waverly, so I stopped in to see him, since we used to golf together every once in a while."

"Okay," I said, hoping the part with the cops would hurry up and get there.

"Well, I had a couple of beers while we talked. It's a nice place. You would have liked it."

Stopping in to see someone was not out of character for my dad, but drinking "a couple of beers" was. I figured maybe he started to loosen up a little after my brother and I got out of his hair.

"Anyway, I start heading home, you know, on the back way that goes through Ionia, the way we used to take when I had to drive you down to the orthodontist."

"Uh-huh."

"Well, as I'm going through Ionia, I really gotta piss. I mean really gotta piss, like now. Nothing's open in Ionia except that one bar, and I don't want to go in there and use their bathroom without buying anything, so I just keep going on my way home. But after I get out of town, I realize I'm not going to make it, so I pull off on that first gravel road. You know, where the Uglums' house is."

"Yeah, Gilmore," I said. I had stopped to pee many times on Gilmore Avenue while drinking with the Uglums' son.

"Well, I'm taking a piss off in the ditch, and a car pulls up behind my truck. It's a state trooper."

"Whoa," I said, wondering what this would mean for my parents' reputation. In our small town, news travels through the beauty salons faster than it does on the internet.

"Yeah," Dad says. "Well, he saw me pissing, which it turns out is actually illegal. Anyway, we start talking, and he smells beer on me and asks me if I'd like to do some roadside maneuvers. You know, touching your nose—"

"Yeah, I know what they are, Dad."

"Yeah. So, I passed 'em, and he asks me if I'd agree to take a breath test, and I figure I better take the breath test, because if you say no—"

"You lose your license for a year. I know, Dad."

"Yeah. Well, I gotta have my license to drive to work, so I take the breath test. I only had a couple of beers, you know."

"Yeah. What'd you blow?" It was killing me.

"Well, I blew a .09."

"Shit," I said.

"And you know, they lowered the limit from .10 to .08, so that's a DUI."

"Jesus Christ, Dad." People in New Hampton would be talking about Joe Leonard by the end of the week, for sure.

"Well, he didn't give me a DUI. He gave me a choice."

"No shit?"

"He said I could either take the DUI or a ticket for indecent exposure, since I was pissing outside."

"Well?" *Please say you took the DUI.*

"Well, I gotta be able to drive to work. What am I gonna do, walk? Have your mother pick me up? I can't do that."

"You took indecent exposure?"

I could already hear the ladies at the hair salons in town: *Did you hear about Joe Leonard, the meat man at Fareway? Got caught out on a gravel road near Ionia, taking a leak. State trooper busted him for indecent exposure.* And that was *if* they heard his side of the story first. If not, he'd be crucified all over the county. DUIs were pretty much a dime a dozen in my hometown. But indecent exposure? You got one, you were marked as a pervert, for sure. My parents were finished in New Hampton.

"So, what? Are you getting a lawyer?" I asked.

"Nah, it's just a fine," he said.

"No shit? How much?"

"Twelve hundred bucks," he said.

"Jeeeeesus Christ," I said. "For indecent exposure?"

"Yep," he said. "A hundred bucks an inch."

Silence. I shook my head.

"You're a fucking asshole, Dad."

Laughter from his end of the phone.

"More like fifty bucks," I said. "You prick."

Louder laughter. It was the sound of the end of his statute of limitations on telling jokes about drunk-driving arrests to his son, who very recently had massively fucked up his life by getting arrested twice for drunk driving. I smiled.

ELEVATION

TIM AND I RACED OUT of Idaho Falls in my old Pontiac, which my parents had driven out to Missoula at the end of the second semester. Near the end of my summer internship at the Idaho Falls *Post Register*, I'd talked Tim into driving down from Missoula for an adventure. We were headed for Ketchum, the town where Ernest Hemingway had been buried after shooting himself in the head with a shotgun in 1961. In the early afternoon, we found his tombstone, covered in coins like a wishing well, and we posed for photos.

After getting groceries, we headed north on Route 75, to the closest town, Stanley, Idaho, population 100, sixty-two miles away. From there, we traced the path of the Salmon River another fifty-five miles to the intersection with Highway 93. Thirty-five miles south of there, we turned onto Birch Springs Road, a rough dirt path that climbs about a thousand feet to the base of Borah Peak.

I'd been working at the *Post Register* in between my semesters at the University of Montana, and one of my coworkers at the newspaper, Jerry Painter, was a real mountain climber. Jerry had said that since Tim and I were planning to go up Borah on a weekday, we'd most likely have the whole mountain to ourselves. But the chatter of twenty or so kids camping at the base of the peak said this was not so on this particular day.

Tim set up his tent, because I still didn't know how to set one up on my own. I helped and tried to watch what he did. He had recommended I buy a sleeping pad to go under my sleeping bag, but I didn't bother, thinking the forty-five dollars I had spent on my Expedition Trails sleeping bag at the army surplus store was enough. Tim had laughed at it when he saw it sitting on the couch in my apartment, because it was so bulky and heavy.

Tim cooked dinner on his backpacking stove, a tiny device that sat on top of a tank of butane the size of a can of cashews. I watched him and then refused when he offered me some food. I was nervous as shit—way too nervous to eat—and I was smoking a cigarette about every twenty minutes. Our destination, Chicken-Out Ridge, was about halfway up the mountain, and a guidebook I'd read had described it as a "knife-edge." According to Jerry, it was a place that could give someone "a quick exit off the mountain." He also told me just to stay as high as possible and I'd be fine. I didn't know what that meant, but that was the least of my long list of anxieties.

Can I handle the altitude? Can I handle climbing fifty-two hundred feet in less than four miles? Is fifty-two hundred feet in less than four miles tough, or is that normal for a climb? I have no frame of reference. Should I really be smoking all these cigarettes right now, the night before I try to haul my skinny carcass up to almost thirteen thousand feet? How high is that, really? Isn't Mount Everest like twenty thousand feet or something? What am I doing here? I've never even read a book about mountain climbing. This is not rational.

Well, quitting smoking a few hours before trying to climb a mountain wouldn't help that much, I reasoned. So I'd just have to take it slow. I walked over to use the pit toilet in the parking lot, and, standing in line with my toilet paper, I chatted up a couple of the kids from the large group. They were from BYU-Idaho, in Rexburg, thirty miles north of Idaho Falls. Their professor had climbed Borah nine times.

Finally, when it was dark, I smoked my last cigarette and crawled into my cheapo sleeping bag next to Tim in the tent. I rolled over on my side, trying to ball up my sweatshirt into a pillow. I tried sleeping on my stomach. Tim, asleep, farted. I tried sleeping on my back. It was quiet. The wind stroked the tent's rain fly. Was I really going to do this?

I tried to sleep on my side again. Nope. Back onto my back. I should have brought a book and a flashlight. Tim farted again. I didn't hear it, but I could smell it.

I hate camping. I wonder if there's a way to do all this outdoor shit and not have to sleep in a tent. What's the point of making yourself miserable to enjoy the outdoors? We could have just gotten up really early in the morning and driven here. No one can possibly get a good night's sleep in these conditions. Maybe Tim was right. I should have bought a sleeping pad. Is that another fart?

I don't know if I'm going to be able to handle this.

━━

At 5 a.m., I gave up the hope of being even halfway well rested and sat up. It was still dark outside the thin nylon wall of the tent. I stuffed my sleeping bag into its stuff sack and went out to put my shoes on. My hiking boots were in a storage shed in Missoula, so I wore my vintage Adidas Marathon Trainers and itchy wool socks. My backpack, crammed full of extra clothes, three liters of water, and some snacks, was heavy—maybe fifteen pounds.

I'd told myself the night before I wasn't going to smoke any cigarettes in the morning, but Tim took so long brushing his teeth and putting in his contact lenses that I figured, the hell with it, I might as well. The sun was beginning to come up, but it was on the other side of Borah Peak, so it was going to be chilly until it could make its way over the top of the huge mass of rock in front of us.

The kids from BYU-Idaho started up the trail ahead of us. I'd been hoping we'd start ahead of them and still have a chance to have the mountain all to ourselves. We walked through the opening in the log fence at the start of the trail and past the sign that said the mountain was named in honor of William E. Borah, a US senator from Idaho from 1907 to 1940, and that it was the tallest mountain in all of Idaho. It was my *first* mountain in all of Idaho.

The trail went up almost immediately. No easy meandering path through the pines, no flowing creek—just a rocky dirt trail pitched at a constant slope. I took big steps.

Tim let me lead for a while, and I charged like I needed to get to the top before 8 a.m. By the time we passed the BYU kids, I was dripping sweat, despite the chilly air. I nodded hello to them and tried to stride ahead like it was the fifth time I'd been up this mountain.

A few minutes later, I prayed the trail would start switchbacking. *There's no way it can be this steep all the way up or I'll never make it.* We ran into another group of hikers and stopped to take our jackets off, then continued on. I let Tim lead, and he set a more conservative pace.

After about ninety minutes, the trees began to thin out and get shorter. We stopped again so Tim could take a shit. I wondered where he could possibly go, but he just started sidehilling across the mountain, perpendicular to the trail, and disappeared. He was back in a few minutes. I wondered if I would ever be able to do that, to walk off into the woods and take a shit like it was nothing. *What did he wipe with? This is black magic.*

The trees ran out, and there was nothing but rock above us. Big gray pieces of jagged rock, all the way to the top. From the road, Borah had looked like it was chiseled out of one big slab of granite, but from halfway up, I realized it was a big pile of boulders. I was surprised my legs had held out so far.

We caught up to an older couple, and Tim started talking to them. I kept quiet, since it was my first time in the wilderness, I guess. They were maybe in their fifties, and they were from Pennsylvania. They had come to Borah on a "highpointing" trip—they were climbing the highest mountain in each of several western states. The day before, they had left New Mexico, where they had climbed Wheeler Peak, and they had driven up to Idaho in a rented RV. They figured they had enough time to climb Borah before they had to catch their flight back to Pennsylvania the next day.

Ahead of us, I could see where hundreds of people had stomped a gravel path up the ridge. Then, as the sun rose over the mountain, the rocks got larger and larger until we had to start using our hands to crawl over huge boulders.

We tried to stay as close to the top of the ridge as possible, weaving back and forth to pick our way across the rock Mohawk with a thousand-foot drop on either side. I realized that if I lost my footing I would tumble down an almost vertical wall of rock and my parents would have to arrange a closed-casket funeral back in Iowa in a few days. I took a deep breath, and thought, *Holy shit.*

In front of us was a snowfield that I'd seen pictures of in all the guidebooks. It was about forty feet across and looked like bad news. How slick was it? Tim went first. To get down to the snow, he had to swing around a big rock and climb backward down to the snow. Then he walked across carefully, but he didn't look worried.

I swung down by my hands off the stacked boulders, hoping not to find out what would happen if I were to slip, then I stepped onto the snow. It was mushy enough to get good footing. Not a good place to fall to the left or the right, but not nearly as scary as the ridge. I stepped carefully, slightly hunched over, ready to dive onto my stomach if I lost my balance. Two guys came up behind us and verified that we had survived Chicken-Out Ridge.

The trail traversed the face of the peak, then disappeared as we started to pick our way through another boulder field. Ten feet in, I was done having fun. It was now all about getting to the top. There was no easy way, so I put my head down and kept going, stopping to rest every minute and a half. Tim got ahead of me and didn't wait, but I didn't mind. *Up, up, up. Jesus Christ.*

Then I heard Tim talking to someone else, and I knew I must be close. I walked up the last few feet and stood atop Borah Peak. The mountain fell away to the east, and I looked out over a frozen sea of rock. I had made it.

I sat, letting the slight breeze blow on my face, sucking on water that didn't even taste good and chewing on tasteless energy bars.

One of the guys who had crossed the snowfield after us offered to take a "hero shot" of us with Tim's camera. We stood together on the summit and smiled in the sun—me with long hair flipping in my face, thinking for sure that this would be the coolest photo I'd ever be in. I couldn't wait to show it to everyone back in Iowa. I looked at Tim, relieved and said, "Well, it's all downhill from here."

I stumbled almost all the way down the mountain. My legs, not prepared for a task one-tenth the magnitude of what we had just done, had nothing left. I nearly tripped onto my face dozens of times, with Tim conveniently far ahead of me. It was steep going up, but at least if I fell going up, I'd stop. Going down was scary. My mouth hung open as I fantasized about a helicopter rescue.

Back in Idaho Falls, Tim and I hit up a fast-food drive-through and went back to my apartment to take turns showering. While Tim was in the bathroom, I called everybody I could think of, acting like, oh, today was just a good day to get caught up on my phone calls. "What have you been up to?" I asked. "Me? Oh, nothing. But my buddy Tim is in town, and we just climbed a twelve-thousand-foot mountain."

Of course, over the phone, no one had any idea how nervous I was the night before, or how miserable I was on the way up, or how clumsy and utterly wiped out I was on the way down. I assumed they pictured me with ice ax in hand, rope around my waist tethering me to earth, at the top of a desolate snow-covered giant, possibly even sporting a beard with icicles hanging off it, maybe planting a tattered American flag at the top.

Safely back at home, I knew I wanted to be a mountain climber—whatever that was.

⊂⊃

A week later, I packed up my apartment, worked my last internship shift at the newspaper, and drove back to Iowa, stopping in Denver to see a friend and hike up 14,433-foot Mount Elbert, Colorado's highest peak. It proved to be no easier than Borah Peak, but at least I'd known more about what to expect.

I drove the fourteen hours back to my hometown in Iowa for a wedding. Weddings were starting to become a sort of regular test of my resolve to stay sober.

I stood with the other groomsmen at the front of the Jericho Lutheran Church way out in the country in northeast Iowa, sweating in my tux, hands clasped in front of me, ponytail tied back. Jarrett was the third generation of his family to get married in that church. He and Angie said their vows, and I tried to stand as motionless as possible. I saw lots of people I knew. I didn't really want to talk to them after the service, not because I didn't like them, but because I didn't know what to say. I snuck out quickly and smoked a cigarette in the hot sun.

For the trip to the reception hall fifteen miles away in Lawler, I boarded a small charter bus with the rest of the wedding party. Everyone cracked open beers like, whew, they were relieved to have that whole thing over with. I watched them drink and loosen up, laughing and joking. I tightened up. Watching people drink was still about my least favorite thing to do. I stared out the window watching the humid countryside go by.

I would not have said it at the time, but this was when I started to close the door on an adult life in the Midwest. It became the place I grew up, no longer home. I wasn't just doing a two-year stint out in Montana; I was gone—too in love with the open spaces to ever think about coming back to Iowa. Even now, I wished I were in Idaho, on a distant mountain ridge where there were no people drinking. Everyone else on the bus had a cold domestic light beer in hand, sweating condensation on the aluminum, or stuffed in a can coozie. I just kept my hands folded on my lap.

Where I grew up, lots of people had a favorite drink, or sometimes only one thing they ever drank. At the bar where I worked, many customers had an allegiance to either Miller Lite or Bud Light, refusing to even drink a free pint of the other stuff when offered. Some grandfathers I knew drank only 7 and 7s; some guys drank only Old Milwaukee when they went fishing. Some people drank only Captain Morgan and Coke when they went out. Over the eight years I drank, I tried almost everything.

One day after I quit, I sat down with a notebook and a pen and tried to remember it all. The list generated a bittersweet nostalgia, like finding a box of old baseball cards I'd collected when I was twelve. The list ran onto two pages, then a third, dozens of brands of whiskey, gin, vodka, and beer, names of cocktails, winding through memories—that four-pack of Olde English 800 while driving to the 1999 Tibetan Freedom Concert, nasty cans of Hamm's beer we'd appropriated from Tony's grandmother's basement when I was seventeen, the eleven White Russians I drank the day after I got my first DUI and drove to Omaha without a driver's license, just a piece of paper saying it had been confiscated and I had nine days left to drive before it was illegal.

For years after I made the list, if I had a minute to myself in a bar or restaurant, I'd scan the beer taps, the glass doors of the coolers, and the racks of liquor behind the bar, and mentally check off all the things I'd drunk before. If I got really into it, I would try to remember how something tasted, like Newcastle or Budweiser. I would often wonder why I did that to myself. But it reminded me of the epic length of that list. *Do you really need a beer? In a short number of years, you had hundreds, probably thousands. You did that. So you don't need another one, or fifty.*

At the reception hall, before dinner was served, Jarrett thanked me for being there, because he knew it was difficult for me to hang out in places where free drinks were served. I told him it was really hard—like you have no idea how hard—but I was glad to do it for his wedding day.

I walked over to chat with my mom and dad, and Mom introduced me to a couple I'd never met before.

"Nice to meet you," I said.

"You live in Montana," the man, named Herman, said.

Yes, I live in Montana. I was prouder than shit to say I lived in Montana. *I have a ponytail full of long curly hair. I live in Montana, and I climb mountains.*

"Tell them about mountain climbing," my mom said.

I had no idea what she wanted me to say. I just said that over the past few weeks I'd climbed a couple of pretty big mountains—Borah Peak in Idaho and Mount Elbert in Colorado. I explained how high they were and how we'd had to leave very early in the morning to avoid afternoon lightning storms.

Herman and his wife nodded and listened, but I could see they had no way of relating to what I said. I might as well have been talking about my recent trip to the moon. I liked the idea of people from back home seeing me as a "mountain climber," but while I was talking to Herman and his wife, I realized that probably nobody from back home had any idea what a mountain climber really was. Not that I had any idea either.

Before the toast, I asked the waitress to please fill my champagne flute with water, not champagne, or to just not fill it at all, thank you. But when I came back from the bathroom, I saw a flute full of champagne sitting in front of my chair just as Jarrett's brothers, co–best men, started their speeches. *Shit.*

The groomsman next to me, David, offered to chug my champagne. After he emptied it, I filled the glass with water, we raised our glasses to the happy couple, and I took a big sip. *Fuck.* There was still champagne in the glass. Not much—less than a quarter ounce, and it was very watered down—but it was the first booze I'd tasted in seventeen months.

My stomach knotted. I didn't know what to do. I set the glass down, took a breath, and moved the glass a foot farther away from me on the table. *There was no champagne in the flute when I poured the water in.*

"What's wrong?" David asked.

"Oh, there was a little sip left in there, and I got a taste of it," I said. "It's okay."

How much champagne could have been hanging on the sides of the glass? I didn't drink more than an ounce of water. But it tasted like alcohol. Did I just fall off the wagon?

No.

I went outside to smoke a cigarette, one of my little sobriety sticks, and I hung on. Maybe this is what people feel like when they've seen a ghost.

For most of the rest of the night, I sat in a folding chair on the edge of the dance floor, drinking water. I was determined to stay until the end—for Jarrett. A breeze drifted in through the window, carrying with it the smell of hog manure, and it reminded me that this was where I was from. I recognized dozens of people on the dance floor, or standing near the bar, drinking cocktails out of plastic cups or beer from cans, and I felt suddenly like they were from another lifetime.

Four years ago, with eight beers in my stomach, I'd have been having the time of my life, catching up with old Dan Crooks, who I hadn't seen in six years, or doing shots with Shawn Hackman, reminiscing about the summer seven years before when we'd been fighting over a girl. (She ended up marrying someone else a couple of years later.) Give me a beer, and then seven more, and I could have been part of all this, possibly even the life of the party.

Now, though, a lot had changed. I was a brooding outsider, most comfortable sitting out on the front steps smoking another cigarette by myself. I was feeling homesick for Montana, or Idaho, or anywhere out West that had a horizon that wasn't flat.

⸏

But back in my hometown, a lot had not changed. My dad decided that while I was home, we were going to build a fence in the front yard, over by the grove of trees that I'd been flicking cigarette butts into each time I'd visited over the past four years. It would be about 110 feet long, requiring eleven ten-foot-wide panels of fence and twelve posts. To dig the two-foot-deep holes for the posts, Dad had a plan: he'd rent a skid loader and use an auger attachment to drill them out. The fact that he had no experience operating one was no deterrent.

"No problem," he said. We would borrow it from Stan, who, in addition to being the skilled owner and operator of New Hampton Auto Body and a sometime Wednesday afternoon golf partner, apparently had a skid loader sitting in his garage.

Stan's price? Eight steaks from my dad's meat case and a few cases of Busch Light.

"Jesus," I said. "Why don't we get him some good beer? The guy's saving you three hundred dollars."

"Because," Dad said, "they don't drink good beer at New Hampton Auto Body. They want Busch Light."

Beer was often used as currency in my hometown. When I was in high school, I used to gamble for it with a twenty-six-year-old guy I worked with. I bought my first car for $500 and two cases of beer from a guy who worked for my dad. Dad once paid a guy a twelve-pack of Miller Lite to grade a fresh pile of gravel on our driveway.

We built the fence, and I painted the whole goddamn thing in one long day, finishing in the dark and aggravating the carpal tunnel I'd given myself designing newspaper pages six days a week all summer.

Those two weeks in Iowa felt too long. There weren't many high school friends left in New Hampton, and my college friends lived too far from Mom and Dad's house. If I'd been a little bored here when I'd been able to drink, I struggled even more when I couldn't drink. I stayed around to maximize the time with my parents before I would drive the thirteen hundred miles back to Montana, and I counted down the days until I could point my car west again.

〜

Before I left, I drove two hours to go see my grandmother.

"You know, Brendan," she said from her cozy kitchen table as we sat down for lunch, "You're the only grandchild I have who's ever driven out here to come visit me." She was my mother's mother, 100 percent Irish, just like my mom. Grandma lived in Emmetsburg, Iowa, a sister city of Dublin, named after the Irish hero Bold Robert Emmet. They had a blarney stone in front of the courthouse, shamrocks painted on the water tower, and a parade every Saint Patrick's Day.

"I know I'm the only one who's driven out to see you," I told Grandma. "That's why I'm your favorite grandchild." I thought of the year and a half when I'd had all the time in the world to visit but I didn't have a driver's license because I got caught driving drunk.

Over the years, Grandma had said to me more than once, "Brendan, you're half-Irish, and that's the only half you need to worry about." She never said, "Being Irish means you've got something to be proud of when you've got nothing else," but I understood it anyway. I think that was why I got the claddagh tattoo on my arm on my one-year anniversary of being sober, after five years of telling people ridiculous things like, "I'm Irish, that's why I drink so much whiskey." I thought about showing her the tattoo. I thought she might like it. I tried to think of a way to bring it up.

Mom didn't ever tell Grandma about my drinking problem, maybe because of my grandfather. Mom always said I reminded her of Grandpa. She'd show me pictures of him when he was young and say, "Look at Grandpa's curly hair. It looks just like yours, doesn't it?" After I went into rehab, Mom never told me I looked like Grandpa.

Grandma and I drank coffee in the kitchen after lunch, and I opened the fridge to get some milk. I saw a six-pack of Michelob Light in there, and I said, "Grandma, what the hell is this? Have you been tossing back a few?"

"Oh, no," she said. "I bought that for you. I thought maybe you could have one or two of those tonight if you want."

"I quit drinking, Grandma," I said. "But thanks anyway."

"Oh," she said. "Good for you."

I decided not to show her the tattoo, because I didn't want to tell her I got it because I grew up to be just like Grandpa.

I drove back to Missoula a week before the start of classes, feeling a warm welcome pulling me the final miles down I-90 through Hellgate Canyon, the town buzzing with energy as thousands of students returned to campus.

The first nice Saturday of the fall, I convinced Tim to take me up Lolo Peak, the 9,096-foot mountain that dominates the sky west of Missoula. It's the first place snow appears in the fall and the last place it melts in the spring. Every time I turned my car southwest onto Brooks Street, it sat right in the middle of my windshield.

After four miles of hiking up through thinning pines, we passed by Carlton Lake, just before the final one-thousand-foot scramble to the summit. I was out of breath but undaunted.

We picked our way up boulders to the summit, where we saw Lisa, a photographer I knew from the campus newspaper, and her dad, who had grown up around Missoula. He reminisced about how they used to drive Jeeps most of the way up the mountain. I introduced Tim to both of them and thought how strange it was to run into someone I knew on top of a peak.

In the summit register, aside from the usual notebook to sign, there was a letter from a guy to a girl. Apparently, their first date was a climb of Lolo Peak, but they had since broken up. The guy wanted the girl back and had left the letter for her, on top of the mountain, in the hopes that she'd find it. About ten people had contributed responses ranging from *You sound like a really nice guy. I hope she comes to her senses* to *You're a moron if you think this is going to get her back. Why don't you try calling her?*

⸏

A few weekends later, I made my first real mistake on a mountain. I was hiking by myself on Trapper Peak, a jagged sawtooth of gray rock just south of Darby, Montana. With no one to talk to, I covered the four miles to the summit far too fast for my lungs to keep my brain supplied with oxygen. I scrambled over boulders to the top, where the mountain's north wall dropped down a thousand feet. Three other people chatted on the summit.

I kept to myself and looked out at the sea of rocky tops fanning out for miles to the west and north. I sat down, ate a Clif Bar, walked around a bit, and finally asked one of the other three folks to take a quick photo of me. Then I started bounding down the boulders, sure I'd be back in Missoula in record time.

Down and down I went, until the rock suddenly became too loose to hold itself under my feet on the steep slope. I stopped. *Where am I?* I had veered off course and gone too far down. *Where was the trail going to show up? Shit.*

Shit shit shit.

Was it to the left or the right? How was I going to find it?

I pulled my map out of my pocket—it was nothing more than a photocopy of a hand-drawn map from an old guidebook page, not the USGS topo map they tell you to learn how to read before venturing into the wilderness by yourself. It was a few curved lines on a page, crude and useless. I was fucked. Lost and fucked.

Take a deep breath. Look around.

I calmed down, turned back uphill, and tried to climb. But the rock was so loose under my feet, I could barely take a step two feet up that didn't slide a foot and a half down.

Okay.

I turned to my left to try to sidehill my way slightly up and to the north.

If I cut across the east face of the peak long enough, I figured, I would cross the trail eventually, since it had to go at least somewhat up and down the mountain. I walked, scanning the mountainside for a trace of beaten soil. I saw nothing.

Mountains are big. You can't just start running down one and expect to magically end up exactly where you parked your car.

Then I saw two people headed up the mountain. A few steps later, I saw the trail. The right trail.

Thank you thank you thank you thank you.

Just below tree line, my head started to pound. I sat down, drank as much water as I could stomach, and hiked the rest of the way down with a sloshing belly.

In the car just outside Hamilton, about an hour from Missoula, my head felt like it was being split by an ax from the inside out. I chugged more water and smoked more cigarettes. I stopped and got a cup of coffee, hoping it was caffeine withdrawal.

No luck.

Aspirin, water, ibuprofen—nothing helped. I wanted to pass out. I knew it had to be altitude sickness. I had climbed Trapper way too fast, going up thirty-eight hundred feet in less than four hours.

I was in bed by 8 p.m.

After that, I gave up on mountaintops until spring. By November, it had started snowing, which made it tough for a guy with no equipment. I didn't even try, figuring I'd need snowshoes ($100) at the very least, and maybe crampons ($80) and an ice ax ($80), not to mention some sort of knowledge of how to not slide to my death off the sides of snow-and-ice-covered peaks. I continued to cling to my packs of cigarettes ($3 each).

The next Tuesday afternoon after Trapper Peak, I stopped by Tim's apartment on my way home from campus. "What have you been up to?" he said.

"Just working on my thesis," I said.

I had been meeting once a week with Clem Work, the head of the graduate program at the School of Journalism, to discuss it. I had kind of decided on a somewhat vague topic: "Newspapers and the Internet." It sucked. I was not looking forward to spending the next seven months researching and writing.

"What's it on?" Tim asked. "Peak bagging?"

Huh.

I poked around the internet before my next meeting with Clem, and we talked through what I might be able to do. I remembered the folks from Borah Peak who said they were highpointers, and I found their club. The founder had died, and as part of his dying wishes, club members were trying to scatter his ashes on the high points of all fifty states, from Britton Hill in Florida to Denali in Alaska. I found another guy who spent all of his spare time obsessing over county high points—interesting out West, but charmingly tedious and even ridiculous in flatter areas, like the golf course in New York City that happened to have the county high point inside its fences, or the county in Illinois where you had to visit dozens of spots to make absolutely certain you'd touched the high point.

Before we closed out the semester and I got on a plane back to Iowa, I was well into the preliminary research for my project: a series of magazine-style articles on peak bagging.

⸻

I was so excited about mountains and writing and the West that I hated to go back to Iowa. Winter was always tough there, especially after Christmas was over and just the dark cold days remained. But I was looking forward to seeing some friends. I flew to Minneapolis, made the ridiculous thirty-minute roundtrip walk through security to get outside for two rapid-fire cigarettes, then back inside before my connecting flight to Rochester, Minnesota, the closest airport to my parents' house.

One of my high school buddies, Robb, called me at Mom and Dad's house and said maybe we should go over to this party at our friend Scott's.

"Sure," I said. "I think I'm pretty solid. Damn near two years sober, albeit white-knuckling it. I can drive you guys around town, at least, make sure you're not driving drunk."

I clutched a Styrofoam cup of Kwik Star coffee and moved uneasily around the party, talking to old friends, who sipped their first or third or fifth beer. I hadn't seen most of the people there in four or five years, and every person I talked to pointed to the cup of coffee.

I'd say, "Yeah, I quit drinking," probably with all the confidence of someone who'd been sober for three days.

This, I began to find out, evoked one of two responses:

1. "Really? Good for you." This was the nice response, but it made me hate— fucking hate—the person who said it. I hated them because they meant well but really had no idea what it was like. Sometimes it came out like I had told them I had decided to cut down on my salt intake or quit eating trans fat.

2. "Yeah, I don't drink too much anymore either." This was worse. *You know who doesn't drink too much anymore? Me. In fact, my entire existence has been dependent on the fact that I have had zero beers in the past year and a half, and will continue to have zero beers for the rest of my goddamn life.*

Keith, however, didn't say either of those things, during what was probably the first conversation we'd had since graduating from high school six years prior. He said, "Yeah, I heard you had some problems down in Cedar Falls. That was probably a good idea."

Thank you, Keith. Thank you thank you thank you. You get it.

After the party, we went to a bar a friend's father had opened after we graduated. Everyone was pretty well on their way to a good time. I ordered water and smoked a cigarette every fifteen minutes.

I had never kept track before, but I couldn't believe how much my friend Bob could drink and not appear drunk. The last time we'd gone out, we had an informal Guinness-drinking contest at a bar in Cedar Falls and I set my couch on fire.

OXYGEN

ANOTHER SUMMER, ANOTHER SATURDAY IN a sweaty tuxedo, watching people drink to celebrate a wedding. This time it was my brother's.

After graduation from UM, I had moved to Arizona to get back together with Amy, patching things up after a couple years of clarity, and missing each other. We were living together in her apartment in Scottsdale, both of us having fun but neither of us quite feeling at home in the sprawling desert city, especially during the summer, when it can hit one hundred degrees at nine thirty every morning. She was working as an aesthetician at a day spa, and I was spending most of my time applying for newspaper jobs, only recently picking up a couple of part-time gigs.

But we were together, and not lonely. Chad's wedding in Wisconsin was hot, but a welcome break from the oven-like Arizona desert.

I was three weeks shy of two and a half years sober, leaving another wedding reception early. On the walk to our hotel room, I passed by a window that looked out on the pool just in time to see Chad jump into the deep end with his tuxedo on, having a blast with his college buddies. I think my mother would have preferred him to drink six fewer beers than he did that night. Even two and a half years later, I would have gladly drunk them for him, especially in the nervous hour leading up to my best man speech at the reception.

⸺

My brother's not an alcoholic. He's never been through any sort of treatment. No one's ever mentioned that he might have some sort of problem with booze. He can drink two beers every night for the rest of his life if he wants to.

We have the same genetics and pretty much the same upbringing, yet he was working a good job, raising a family, buying a house, and living a contented life in a Midwest town. Meanwhile, I was a tortured recovering alcoholic trying to figure it all out in the backcountry out West.

Chad had a hell of a time quitting smoking. He took his drinking too far at least a few times, too, and got arrested for drunk driving once in Minnesota. What makes me the certified alcoholic and not him? Is there some sort of drinks-per-week average that I exceeded? How close was he to that average?

I'm sure Chad drank too much during his college years, as most of my friends did. Hell, before he and Meg had kids, Chad still cut loose every once in a while and had to call Meg to pick him up at the bar.

But maybe he could put it down. Maybe he didn't feel like he had to finish the bottle, or the night. Maybe he could drink too much without being an asshole and wrecking everyone's lives around him.

We had never been that alike, as brothers go. He was good at video games, while I dove into books. Every once in a while, he would skillfully work his way through the levels on games like *Mike Tyson's Punch-Out!!*

or *The Legend of Zelda*, then hand me the controller and let me try to finish off the game. Sometimes I did okay, but mostly I sucked. Classes, especially reading and writing, were easy for me, and football and basketball were easy for him. He had a steady girlfriend, and his social schedule mostly revolved around her, while I struggled through high school relationships and mostly hung out with my troublemaking friends.

After college, our paths diverged even further. He got married, got a job with a big company, bought a house, and started having kids. He built things in his spare time and started house remodeling. I kept searching, never finding the right "good job" my sensible upbringing and education should have led me to. I never saved much money, never drove a decent car. The only "nice" things I had were photos and stories from the places I'd been and the things I'd done.

So what makes people so different when they grow up in the exact same environment? Sometimes I think that the shock of having to quit drinking when I was twenty-three might have been the most formative thing that ever happened to me. It forced reinvention right when I should have had the beginning of my life figured out: *I am a guy with a marketing degree. I live in northeast Iowa. I like to drink beer. This is my path in life. I know who I am. This is what I do.* But then all of a sudden it wasn't who I was. Maybe if you find yourself questioning all those things at twenty-three, you never stop questioning them, and never settle on an answer. Or maybe I'm just really bad at growing up and that's my pretentious way of rationalizing it.

Back in Phoenix, I tried to get a handle on my new job as a sales floor associate at REI, the best gig I could land with my new master's degree in journalism. For three months, I had applied to every newspaper in the metro area, finally applying at REI after hearing nothing back. And on the sales floor, you can get lucky and avoid hard questions from customers for only so long.

I stood there looking at a dozen sleeping bags hanging from the ceiling, some guy asking me what the difference was in the insulation between this one and that one. I didn't know. I felt around for the tags and hoped that some information would pop into my head. Or that the guy would just decide he liked the blue one because it was blue, and it would do just fine for his upcoming backpacking trip to the bottom of the Grand Canyon. Sweat drenched the armpits of my T-shirt under my green vest.

I didn't feel like I exactly belonged on the staff at the Phoenix REI store, with its thirty-foot climbing wall, huge inventory of mountain bikes, racks of sleeping bags, and tents and backpacks made of space-age ultralightweight, ultratough, and ultrawaterproof materials. All I knew about outdoor gear was that I needed to acquire some.

My first six weeks, I was scared to death. I thought it was only a matter of time before someone outed me for the poseur I was. I learned quickly about sleeping bags, tents, sleeping pads, backpacks, stoves, and water filtration systems—partly because I was nervous about talking to customers and partly because I was excited to buy a bunch of gear as soon as I had enough money.

My direct opposite at the shop was a guy named Brian who knew everything about outdoor gear and could so authoritatively tell you which tent was the best that you wanted to buy two of them. Brian had two jobs, one at REI and one at a web hosting company, so his free time was scarce and well utilized. He was fond of driving two hours up I-17 to Flagstaff at ten at night and hiking by headlamp to the top of 12,633-foot Humphreys Peak, just so he could get some altitude training for his upcoming Mount Rainier trip. He was a hard-ass. It was with some trepidation that I mentioned to him that we had the same Saturday off. He suggested we climb Humphreys.

Our jaunt up Humphreys would be Brian's sixth or seventh in the past two months. Two nights prior, it had snowed on the San Francisco Peaks for the first time that season. We heard it was "a light dusting," but the trail was piled with white slush, warming in the morning sun. Brian set a quick pace, slightly uncomfortable for me, and before long, we were nearly above tree line. The few remaining trees at that altitude were crusted with clumps of snow, more white than green.

At the saddle between Agassiz Peak and Humphreys, the wind started drilling us. On the east side of the peaks, the plains were a dry green and brown. We had emerged from the trees into a polar landscape sculpted by wind. A trail sign had foot-long icicles growing at ninety-degree angles from its sides. This was going to be cold.

I was sucking air. On the ridgeline to the summit, Brian got a couple hundred feet ahead of me, and my head started to thump with a thick, blunt pain. Altitude sickness—again. I tried to breathe deep and force oxygen into my lungs. I slowed down, and Brian went farther ahead, maybe a couple hundred feet. I knew I should turn around and go back down.

What could happen to me, this high, in conditions this bad? Was my body shutting down, or just getting sick? My hands were going numb, my pant legs frozen to my boots. Vomit sat just below my throat, ready to rise.

I plodded on, stopping every ten steps to take three deep breaths, then stopping every five steps. The wind blew harder, knocking me off balance. I was angry at the wind; I wanted to put my fist through it. I counted off ten more shuffling steps. *If I could just throw up, I'd feel better.* Then ten more steps.

I was at the top. Brian squatted in a makeshift windbreak, a couch-size hole dug out of the snow. He took a quick photo of me with my disposable camera, and we started down.

Back in Scottsdale that evening, it was seventy-five degrees as I smoked cigarettes on the deck in sandals.

⸺

I got my first newspaper job in the fall, at a tiny suburban twice-weekly paper. I wore business casual clothes, even though I hated them, and wrote small stories, collected event calendar listings, and laid out pages of newsprint.

Amy continued at the day spa, helping the women of Scottsdale feel a little more beautiful. It was a shock to live in Scottsdale after I'd spent the past two years in Missoula, where every street seemed to end at a mountain or a river instead of a golf course.

I kept the part-time job at REI, pouring my paychecks from the store into discounted outdoor gear. I gradually stockpiled everything I'd need for backpacking and peak bagging.

I had never considered rock climbing, but once in a while, I would glance over at the climbing gear and ropes. One day at the store, a coworker told me he was headed to Mount Whitney in the spring to do the *Mountaineers Route*. I asked him what the point was of doing a technical route when there was a perfectly good trail up the back. I just wanted to be in the mountains, not haul all that metal stuff around to climb vertically.

⸺

Back in Iowa for the holidays, I pulled a microwave-size box out from under the Christmas tree: *To Brendan, From Chad.* Inside was a climbing rope, sixty meters long, blue, black, and green weave, BlueWater Enduro, designed to stretch and absorb the fall of a climber. It wasn't neatly coiled or shrink-wrapped, like the ones we sold at REI; it was just piled into the box. Standard fare for Christmas gifts between brothers—we care, but let's not get too mushy about it.

What the hell am I going to do with this? Might as well be a sweater.

"It's a good rope," Chad said. He had bought it a year ago, before deciding he wasn't going to be a rock climber, at least not outside a climbing gym. It had never been used.

I didn't think I needed it either. I was starting to fall in love with the exhilaration of the high-altitude environment—the wind blowing across rocky ridges, the exposure to the elements, and the grit it took to keep pushing forward and up despite exhaustion. Yet I felt content to stay on terrain that my hiking boots could stick to.

To me, the rope seemed like a regift, like, *Hey, I was cleaning out my garage, and I found this rope. I'm not using it, so here's your Christmas present.* I had never climbed with a rope before and didn't think I was interested in trying it anytime soon. I'm from Iowa. We're sensible people. We don't go looking for new, crazy things in our late twenties. We settle down into good jobs and start getting the pieces in place to raise a family—reliable car, decent house, 401(k). We don't become adrenaline junkies or what-ever the hell you call people who go rock climbing. Still, I wasn't going to not take the rope back to Phoenix with me. It was, after all, a $200 rope.

I mumbled thanks, like you do, and we moved on, watching my mom open her gift from my dad, a pair of jeans with a hundred dollars in the pocket.

⸺

When you talk about things that change your life, you think about hav-ing kids, finding Jesus, getting a job opportunity that skyrocketed your career, stuff like that. You don't think about some crap your brother threw in a box three days before Christmas. But I suppose I should have known by then not to expect the predictable.

I could have stayed in Cedar Falls, Iowa, after college, drinking four or five nights a week at Toads and Berk's, watching my belly get bigger. I could have made excuses about my two DUI convictions, about how the cops had it out for me or how I was unlucky. I could have hit on college girls until my mid-thirties, maybe convinced one of them to marry me. Maybe that would have been okay.

But I couldn't help but think about this one saying that people like. Part of it is attributed to Henry David Thoreau, but the second half is likely a paraphrasing of something Oliver Wendell Holmes wrote.

> Most men lead lives of quiet desperation and go to the
> grave with the song still in them.

I heard that and I wondered if I was one of those people who was headed to the grave with the song still in them. I think I was on my way there at twenty-three. There was passion inside, but I didn't know where to direct it, so I just poured whiskey on it. Now I was bouncing off the walls, pacing around a tiny room.

Still, I thought I was pretty happy. I was about to turn twenty-six, I lived with Amy, and I could pay my rent, if not my student loan payments, with my first newspaper job. I hadn't had a drink in almost three years. I felt strong.

But I wasn't happy. I wasn't solid, or confident. Sobriety was like an itchy sweater I had been forced to wear to some formal event. I was treading water in life, rudderless, coasting. I didn't know what I was or what I was about. I knew only two things: I couldn't drink anymore, and I wanted to write.

And then I opened that box. That rope would change my life.

⸺

Most of the guys who worked in my department at REI climbed. They talked about it a lot, and I learned that the "rock" in "rock climbing" is silent if you know what you're talking about. They all climbed a couple of times a week at AZ on the Rocks, the climbing gym in Scottsdale, and went to Flagstaff or Queen Creek for real rock whenever they got a chance.

They knew the difference between the ropes we sold, not to mention the shoes and the carabiners and all the other hardware. The sixty-dollar Black Diamond cams had value, but to me, they might as well have been fishing tackle.

My coworkers John, Trevor, and Dustin had said to me, "You should go climbing with us," like guys at the golf course wanting me to join a threesome for a round. Golf wasn't scary. But climbing?

I took my Christmas gift rope back to Phoenix, and when I mentioned it to Dustin, he said it was a really good rope. With that big expense out of the way, he said, I might as well get the rest of the gear and he'd teach me to climb. So I bought climbing shoes, which looked like ballet slippers with supersticky rubber on the bottom, a harness, and a belay device, as well as ten carabiners I didn't know how to use.

Dustin and I met after work at Camelback Mountain, which was right in Phoenix and happened to have a few easy climbing routes. He taught me the basics—how to rappel down a rope, how to belay someone who was climbing, and how to communicate with my partner.

After a few weeks of climbing with Dustin, I tried my first lead climb—clipping the rope to the rock as I went up. The stakes are raised when leading climbs: If the leader falls, he falls below the last place he clipped the rope to the wall, and most of the time farther, sometimes as far as twenty or thirty feet before the rope catches him.

This beginner 5.8 route wasn't difficult until I was almost at the top. After climbing up to the second-to-last bolt, thirty feet off the ground, I couldn't work up the nerve to attempt the final move. I hung there, staring at the rock above me, knowing my arms couldn't pull me up and over the lip to the top. And if I fell trying it, I'd whip in a ten-foot arc and slam into the wall.

I was scared. I sat right next to the safety of the bolt, where I couldn't fall more than a foot or so, and talked myself out of it. I yelled to Dustin to let me down.

Back on the ground, I knew I wasn't good enough. I had climbed, and led, even, but quit when it got scary. I hadn't risked anything.

⸻

My third anniversary of getting sober arrived. I didn't plan to celebrate, but Amy baked me a cake in the shape of a giant beer. We ate it and laughed. I felt good, and kind of proud. Three years ago, I was still reeling from waking up in jail. Three years before that, I had probably put another hundred-dollar bar tab on my credit card and missed my Friday morning class.

Three years sober and I was a little more solid, but I still wasn't quite sure what to do when people asked me if I wanted to go get a beer and I often divulged too much of my personal history when turning down their invitation. I decided to go climbing again, determined to push myself a little more.

It was my idea to go, but I knew I wanted to *have climbed* more than I actually wanted to go climbing. I was nervous on the drive out with Nate, a coworker from REI, and then on the hike up to Pinnacle Peak. I secretly hoped we wouldn't find the routes we were looking for.

But we found a route, and Nate offered me the lead. I said sure.

Getting to the first bolt took all the self-control I had. The rock seemed featureless; all that held me was my fingertips and the friction from the toes of my shoes, which felt ready to slip at any second. I clipped the first bolt, assuring that I at least wouldn't plummet all the way to the ground if I did slip.

Above the bolt, where if I slipped I'd fall until the rope ran out and stopped me, I started to panic. I hyperventilated quietly. I couldn't go up, and I couldn't see any holds to try to climb down. I wanted to cling to something secure, anything, but there was nothing.

"Breathe," Nate said from the ground. Because I wasn't breathing.

When my legs began to shake, I instantly wanted to be in bed spooning my girlfriend or sitting out on my deck smoking cigarettes, anywhere but on that goddamn featureless rock, about to fall who knows how far. My hands were soaked, but I couldn't move either of them to dip into the bag of chalk hanging from my waist.

This is insane. If I can get down, I never want to climb again. It's not for me. I don't have the balls for it.

Then I fell.

I slid down the face of the rock, clawing at it, trying to stop myself, breaking my fingernails as all the air disappeared from my lungs.

The rope caught me after about ten feet, and I finally followed Nate's advice and breathed. My shoulders unclenched as Nate lowered me the rest of the way to the ground, maybe eight or ten feet. I untied from the rope, he tied in, and I belayed him as he led the pitch. He made it look easy, gracefully finding tiny holds and moving up the rock. He wasn't scared.

He set up the belay at the top, and I followed. From his top belay, I wouldn't fall more than a foot if I fell. The climbing was difficult, but not that hard. I was a little embarrassed about my freak-out. I was still happy it was over. I still didn't want to go climbing again. We drove to a restaurant and ate cheeseburgers.

While shopping for groceries with Amy a few days later, I bought some off-brand orange juice in a one-gallon jug. By the time we got it home in the trunk of the car, the jug had started to swell up. By the time I got it inside the kitchen, the jug was so swollen it almost wouldn't stand up on its now-round bottom.

I unscrewed the lid to let some of the pressure out and poured myself a glass. I began drinking in large gulps. I didn't notice a funny smell, although there probably was one, because it turned out the orange juice tasted like it was full of alcohol. It must have been fermenting somehow, there in the store cooler. My heart jumped when I tasted it.

"Holy shit!" I yelled, dropping the glass on the kitchen table.

"What?" Amy asked.

"This orange juice has alcohol in it," I said. "It tastes exactly like a fucking screwdriver."

My heart pounded, way too fast for someone innocently trying to get his recommended daily allowance of vitamin C.

My freshman year in college, my brother had given me a recipe for home-brewed hard apple cider. I had skipped the part in the directions that had said to periodically relieve the pressure in the cider jug, and it had exploded in my closet, waking my roommate and me in the middle of the night.

I had somehow failed to see the parallel here, or notice that the orange juice was three days past its expiration date.

I explained this to Amy.

"Did you just fall off the wagon?" she asked.

I don't know, did I? Jesus.

"I don't think so," I said. "I'm pretty sure it doesn't count if it's accidental."

They'd never covered anything like this in treatment, and I never went to AA meetings to ask other people what they thought. I didn't have any friends in recovery. But even accidental exposure to alcohol scared me.

I avoided beer cheese soup, Jack Daniels barbecue sauce, beer brats and tiramisu, which I had tasted for the first time while eating dinner with my brother during my first year of sobriety.

Not eating tiramisu made sense, because it actually contains and tastes like liquor. Those little liquor candies, too. The Jack Daniels barbecue sauce thing made me feel a little ridiculous, but I still couldn't bring myself to buy it, or even hold the bottle in my hand in the supermarket.

⸺

After eleven months in Phoenix, Amy and I left for Denver to be closer to the mountains. Nick, my old roommate, had left his first office job in Iowa and moved to Colorado to work as a ski lift operator at Breckenridge in the winters, then settled in Denver and convinced me it was the place to be with a pitch about the three hundred annual days of sunshine the Front Range supposedly had. On our way to Colorado, Amy and I spent a week in Moab, Utah, in the heart of desert canyon country. We rented a cheap cabin at the Lazy Lizard, a hostel at the south end of town, spending our days in Canyonlands National Park and our evenings in Arches. I remembered Edward Abbey's words, from his book *Desert Solitaire*, about the stark beauty of the desert, and tried to capture in my camera lens the sun and the long shadows on the rock formations at Park Avenue, Courthouse Towers, the Organ, Balanced Rock, the Windows, and Chesler Park.

On our last day in Moab, we hiked around the Fisher Towers. We watched three climbers slowly make their way up *Ancient Art*, a route famous for a twenty-foot walk across a narrow ledge hundreds of feet off the deck, and up to the summit tower, a twisted glob of muddy red sandstone with hardly enough room to seat one person on top.

⸺

On the drive back to the cabin, I remembered that I had signed up for a rock-climbing class the first semester of my freshman year in college. I had missed the first class because it didn't meet at the indoor rock wall in the rec center, where I'd thought it would. I had called the instructor to ask him where I should go for the second session, and he explained that I couldn't take the class after missing the first—they had covered too much for me to catch up.

I dropped the climbing class and took weight training instead. Then I spent the next four years getting drunk and the next two years after that in Montana trying to figure out who I was without booze, and didn't discover climbing until I was twenty-six, nearly eight years after I missed that first rock-climbing class at the University of Northern Iowa.

I wondered out loud in the car, if things had been just a little different my first year of college, would I have seen Moab earlier in my life, fallen in love with its rafting-mountain-biking-climbing-four-wheel-drive soul, its red rock desert backdrop, and its dirtbag ethics, and perhaps moved there and become a climbing guide or a rafting guide?

Amy and I took showers at the Lazy Lizard and split a plate of nachos at the Moab Brewery. And as the sun dropped over the Moab Fault, I was proud and grateful that I had ever made it to Moab at all. After all, if things *had* been just a little different, I could have still been drinking beer and nursing impotent daydreams from a barstool in Iowa, or serving a mandatory prison sentence for my third drunk-driving arrest. Now, we were moving to Denver.

⸺

My first summer in Colorado was straight out of the lyrics from "Rocky Mountain High." Just like the guy in John Denver's song, I moved there in the summer of my twenty-seventh year, comin' home to a place I'd never been before. I went as high as I could as often as I could.

For our first hike in Colorado, Amy and I picked a seven-mile loop that summited three fourteen-thousand-foot peaks: Mount Democrat, Mount Lincoln, and Mount Bross. I was near vomiting almost the entire time thanks to another bout of altitude sickness. It finally subsided in the last half mile back to the car.

⸺

By the end of the year, I'd climbed—mostly with Nick—ten mountains. I'd put almost three hundred miles on my hiking boots, hiking, climbing, and scrambling fifty-four thousand feet of elevation. I had slept on mountainsides and had drunk from mountain lakes full of melted alpine snow that had been filtered through rocks. I'd seen moose, elk, and, once, a porcupine, and gotten close enough to touch mountain goats and marmots.

I was a mountain man, as far as I knew. I'd become the person on top of a rocky peak as the camera zooms out to show infinite waves of mountains, strong, courageous, wild.

DOUBT

ONCE I OPENED *A Million Little Pieces*, a book about a guy going to rehab, I couldn't put it down. I loved James Frey instantly and intensely. The extremes of his addictions were far above mine: I mouthed off to cops; the cops beat him down with batons. I got beat up twice; he beat a man so badly he may have killed him. No question he could drink me under the table, even with the coke and the weed and the gasoline he was sniffing. I admired his consumption, his depravity, his addiction, and his pain. So much so that I started to wonder if I'd really had a problem when I quit, three years and four months ago. *Should I have even quit?*

My cousin Dan quit drinking when he was twenty-one. He told me this when I was eighteen, and I thought he was nuts. His dad, George, my dad's brother, worked at a slaughterhouse and meatpacking plant his whole life and was one of those guys who had a few beers after work, no big deal. Five or six beers, hang out, watch a little TV—no problem. Didn't make anybody unhappy, never got arrested, never really took it too far. I figured since his dad had kept it under control, Dan probably did too.

I never asked Dan what made him think he needed to quit drinking. But I always found myself justifying my own choice, as if I owed people this explanation. Sometimes they asked, so I told them. Sometimes they didn't ask, and I told them anyway, because it was such an odd thing to do in your twenties, not drink. I just assumed they were wondering: *Are you Mormon? Do you just smoke weed instead? Are you straight edge? Or are you just weird?*

⌐⌐

My friend Jayson, one of my best friends and most enthusiastic drinking partners from college, came to visit Amy and me in July, a couple of months after we'd gotten settled in Denver. Jayson had clawed his way up to a director position in the Iowa Democratic Party after growing up with dyslexia and an absent father in a broken home, his mom raising six kids on her own. He survived an adolescence in the tough river town of Burlington, Iowa, and earned everything he ever got. Jayson had been maced by the cops, handcuffed and pushed around, and could scrap his way out of a pack of hyenas.

"Do you really think you had that bad of a problem, Leonard?" asked Jayson, the guy I always think of when I miss having beers with my buddies. "I mean, you weren't any worse than I was back then."

I defended my sobriety, all three years and five months of it. But inside, I wondered the same thing. I missed Jayson, and I missed the smile on his face when I'd walk into Toads or the OP and meet him for the first beer of the night, sitting on barstools, doing shots with the bartender, believing we would never die.

That version of me did die, and Jayson had also changed. He was more responsible, fun, outgoing, positive, enthusiastic. I became a recluse, a cynic, unstable, depressed, old. I missed my friends.

On the last night Jayson was in town, our neighbor threw a mojito party. Out of fifty people in his backyard, I was the only one not drinking. I smoked cigarettes and met a couple of people. Jayson, of course, was a big hit. *If I did decide someday that it was okay to have a couple of beers, what would happen?*

I'd walk into a bar and order a Guinness, or maybe just a Budweiser. I'd have two beers, maybe three. *Got to do it right this time, not get too crazy.* That'd be on a Friday night, maybe happy hour somewhere. I'd go home afterward, kind of proud that I could stop at two or three, but with a tinge of sadness that I couldn't just sit there and keep happy hour going until 2 a.m.

The next week, maybe I'd do the same thing, only on Thursday night. *Hell, everybody starts slacking on Friday anyway, right? Thursday's the real start of the weekend.* Three beers, though. Maybe four at the most. *Got to take it easy.*

Friday, I'd probably try to go out again. Three, maybe four beers. *Hell, maybe five or six, since it's the weekend and all, right?* I'd get a pack of smokes, too. I only smoke when I'm having a couple of beers.

I wouldn't go out on Saturday, though. *Three days in a row, no way.*

By the third week, I'd probably get reasonably drunk—not like the old days, but enough that I'd be a little stumbly and I'd yell at people in the street to draw attention to myself. This is probably the point of no return. Three months after that first beer, tops, and I'd be a total piece of shit again. Next thing you know, I'd be fifty with cirrhosis. I wonder if anybody would still be around to care.

On Labor Day, I quit eating meat for good. Seemed like the right thing to do, for environmental reasons, and for animals. I quit smoking on the same day, for probably the fortieth time in the past two years. I'd gotten a job at a division of the *Rocky Mountain News* when we moved to Denver, and I'd had a few informal "meetings" with my new boss when we went out for cigarette breaks, but other than that, it was hard to see any positives to smoking anymore. Along with the high altitude and the dry air in Denver, smoking was making me miserable. I was always thirsty, I usually had a headache, and it just wasn't fun anymore.

Two months later, Amy got sick of me saying, "Maybe I could just smoke a couple cigarettes a day," or "Just when I have coffee," or blah blah blah.

"Why don't you just go buy some cigarettes and get it out of your system?" she said.

Wow. She would never say that about beer.

So I did.

Down at the corner store on Colfax and Gilpin, a block away, I bought a pack of Marlboro Ultra Lights, convinced that since I hadn't been smoking lately, my throat wouldn't be able to handle anything stronger. I sat on the top step of the porch stairs and lit a cigarette, sucking on the filter and wondering if it would feel as good as I had daydreamed about twenty times a day.

It didn't. It was as tasty as a bite of Styrofoam, empty. I went inside, disappointed that I had just thrown two pure months of nonsmoking down the drain.

An hour later, I went back out onto the porch and smoked one more cigarette in the dark, out of a sense of duty to the four dollars I'd paid for the pack. I burned it down to the filter, sucking down all the smoke, all the chemicals, and wishing for a big rush of nicotine to slide into my blood.

But it didn't happen. I stubbed the butt out, flipped open the box, looked at the eighteen full cigarettes staring back at me in the dark, and walked down the steps to the sidewalk.

I stood the pack right in the middle of the sidewalk so someone would see it and pick it up. I had done this ten times before, on this same spot on the sidewalk, every time I figured I was going to quit for good. Then someone came along and picked up the pack, taking it away, sometimes finding five smokes, sometimes twelve. This time it was eighteen.

⌐

I had smoked for six years, starting back when you could still smoke in bars in Iowa. I'd told myself that if I was getting all that secondhand smoke anyway, I might as well get some firsthand. Like alcohol, it had quickly become an addiction, but I never had a rock-bottom moment that shocked me into quitting, like I did with alcohol. Smoking was a crutch, a safety valve I relied on whenever I felt uncomfortable. Eventually, I just did it because I felt like crap if I didn't. That is the end of the fun phase of all addictions: maintenance. I tried gradually decreasing the number of cigarettes I smoked per day, then I tried nicotine patches, and both failed. Finally, I found the magic trick: cutting it out cold turkey.

I joked with my mom about my career as a quitter—first alcohol, then meat, then smoking—saying maybe it was some sort of adulthood phase for me.

She emailed me a story:

Like many kids, you were comforted in your toddler years by a special blanket and sucking your thumb. You had a green blanket that I had replaced the binding on several times.

Early in the summer after your third birthday, you came to me and said: "Mom, when I think that I am three years old and still suck my thumb, it just makes me sick!"

That night, when I tucked you into bed, I found the green blanket folded on a chair in your room. You associated the green blanket with your thumb and knew by putting the blanket away, your thumb would be less enticing.

A short time later, you became very sick with a high fever and strep throat. In an attempt to comfort you, I tried to give you the green blanket. You refused it, thinking you might start sucking your thumb again.

When I walked out the front door the next morning, I glanced over to the spot on the sidewalk. Sure enough, the pack of cigarettes was gone. That was the last cigarette I ever smoked. But just to make sure it would be, I started training to run the inaugural Colfax Marathon, which started six months later.

⸺

One January day at the newspaper office, under the Cubicleville fluorescent lights and white silence that seemed to numb any ambition to actually work, I took another one of those two-minute mental breaks from writing sentences and creating hyperlinks to click around the internet. I found a news story about James Frey. He'd admitted to embellishing some details in his memoir. *Mother. Fucker.* My heart sank.

Maybe he wasn't the grizzled tough guy he'd said he was. Maybe he'd never stood up to anyone. It was likely, really likely, that he hadn't had a root canal without anesthetic. I had aligned that experience with the time I'd had the wires in my jaw taken out and had declined a general anesthetic, opting instead for twenty shots of novocaine; I'd laughed at myself in the rearview mirror as I'd tried to smoke a cigarette with numb lips on the drive back to my house.

He'd said he did eighty-seven days in jail, when really it was no more than a few hours. I spent a grand total of nine days in three jails, only 216 hours, but I sure didn't walk around acting like it had been six months.

Fucking James Frey, you let me down. I bought your book for my mom so she could understand me. I recommended it to friends. And the guy in your story wasn't who you made him out to be.

"Well, it's still a good story," my mom said when I told her to not bother finishing the book. "It's just a story."

"No, it wasn't, Mom," I said. "Unless you were . . . Never mind."

I had started this whole thing without a hero or a role model, anyway.

UP

"TRUST YOUR FEET," THE GUIDE said. "Your legs are way stronger than your arms, so walk up the rock. Don't try to pull yourself up with your hands."

More than a year after I had said I'd never rock climb again, Nick and I took a class from a guide in Colorado Springs. Our instructor brought us to Garden of the Gods, a valley of three-hundred-foot red sandstone fins and pinnacles sitting at the foot of Pikes Peak. He took it slow, focusing on technique. He showed us how to make the sticky rubber on our shoes cling to the rock on even the smallest features, taught us to find good footholds and move carefully up the rock. And he reminded us to breathe.

Maybe he was a better teacher than my buddies in Phoenix, or maybe I was finally humble enough to really listen, but afterward I felt ready to go out and climb. I bought a couple more pieces of hardware and some guidebooks, and Nick and I headed out. We started with the places where we could walk up the back side of the rock, anchor the rope at the top, and climb the pitch with a rope from above and very minimal risk.

A month and a half of that and I was really ready to lead.

We started at Red Rock Canyon in Colorado Springs, on a not-even-close-to-vertical route. I took it slow and easy, making sure to do everything right. Clipping a carabiner to the rope the wrong way could leave me basically unprotected if I fell, sending me all the way to the ground.

⸺

In a few weeks, I was leading intermediate routes, climbing at the upper limit of my ability, and scaring the shit out of myself on a weekly basis. I was incredibly scared of heights, and of falling.

But I couldn't stop. When I climbed, I concentrated only on climbing—keeping enough friction between my hands and feet and the rock to stay on it, forty or sixty feet off the ground. Everything else fell away outside of the tunnel of my vision.

In climbing, if you make a mistake, you can die. If your partner makes a mistake, you can die. Even if everything goes right, you can still fall, and during the one or two seconds after you come off the wall and you're hanging in space, you hope or pray the rope will hold the force of your fall and your partner will hold the rope. For a second, you are dying, just before the rope catches and you slam into the rock, thankful for the workmanship of the rope maker and the accountability of your best friend. You always knew he would take a punch for you, but right now you're just glad he's willing to competently hold tight to a climbing rope when you're tied to the other end, way up there.

⸺

Four months after I learned to climb Garden of the Gods, I was hanging onto a vertical slice of granite called the Fin with my fingertips and the toes of my climbing shoes. I was about twenty-five feet off the ground, forty feet from the top, on a route called the *Edge of Time*. If I slid over to my right and peered around the rock, I would have a beautiful view of the Diamond on the east face of Longs Peak, five miles away as the crow flies. I couldn't see that view, however, because I was about to fall.

I was a few feet above the first bolt on the route, climbing above my ability. In addition, I was not mentally prepared to try this route, a sand-bagged 5.9 climb in an area where I'd never climbed before. The hand-holds and footholds I relied on were tiny, sloped, barely helpful nubs sticking out of the rock. The next move I made could send me peeling off the wall. No one could do anything to help me.

I went for it, upsetting the delicate balance of friction I had with my left hand and my two feet. I fell, mostly straight down, crashing through a pine tree, bashing my elbow on the rock. My throat sucked in a scream as I flew free.

Nick tried to hold the rope and prevent me from hitting the ground, but he was sucked into the wall himself, and I fell a couple more feet.

Then I stopped falling, with my heels about six inches off the ground. Nick and I ended up right next to each other, two guys coursing adrenaline, looking at a wall, both scared and relieved.

"Holy shit," he said after a second.

My elbow was bleeding, staining my long-sleeve shirt. My pants were ripped where a tree branch caught them and took a three-inch long gash out of my ass cheek. Both stung. But I didn't hit the ground.

We talked about what happened and decided Nick should try to lead the rest of the route, since the first bolt was already clipped. I anchored myself to a small tree, and he roped up and started climbing, making it past the tough part where I'd peeled off.

About fifty feet off the ground, almost at the fourth bolt, he started to get fatigued, badly, to the point where he didn't think he could hang on. I told him to start climbing down, because he was easily eight feet above the third bolt, which meant if he fell, he'd fall sixteen feet before the rope stopped him. He tried to downclimb and got almost four feet closer to the third bolt before he sailed off the rock in an arc, away and to the left, slamming into the wall with his hip as the rope caught him and stopped his descent.

I could see that this was the most scared Nick had been in his entire life. For a second, he thought he was going to die. Neither Nick nor I knew how to properly fall while climbing.

I lowered him down to the ground, shaken. Then I gave the route one more shot, not thinking I'd make it very far. I made it past the spot where I'd fallen, then past the second and third bolts, when I really started to panic. I was easily forty feet off the ground. I had no reason to believe that every part of the system wouldn't work—the rope, my harness, the bolts, the quickdraws holding the rope to the bolts, Nick and his belay, and the anchor holding Nick to the tree—but I was still hyperventilating. *Shit shit shit.*

The fifth bolt was a piton, hammered into the rock God knows how many years ago, and what, about a fifty-fifty chance it was worth a shit and would actually hold a fall or rip out of the rock and let me free-fall another thirty feet? *Looks solid. I guess it looks solid. I don't really know.*

I slowly crept up the wall. The climbing wasn't hard, just high and airy. I tried to breathe deep, yoga style. I clipped the piton and took a deep breath. Twelve more feet to the top.

Easy climbing again, but still frightening. I slowly made moves, shifting my feet to the next hold only when completely sure I could make it. A fall from there would only drop me ten or fifteen feet, but it would still be fifty feet off the ground. If the piton actually held the weight of the fall, that is. It could be a thirty-footer if it didn't.

At the top, I clipped in to the rappel bolts, and my butt unclenched.

"I'm off," I yelled down to Nick. I ran the rope through the rappel bolts, and he lowered me to the ground. My heart glowed with adrenaline, and I laughed.

⸺

There is nothing else when you're climbing. There isn't room for the mind to wander. No bills, no angry boss, no girlfriend, no debt, no depression, no heartbreak, no expectations, no questioning your life choices or career, no success and no failure; there is just staying on that rock and concentrating on safe, upward movement.

On the rock, I'm still an addict, but I don't crave a beer or a cigarette, not even at the top. I want to push myself to the top, then back down, then climb more—a tougher route, a tougher one, until my calves cramp up and my fingers are too weak to tug on my shoelaces.

This was it.

"Be careful," my mother always says when I mention climbing. She never said that before I went on a drinking binge. Is it more foolish to risk your life or risk wasting your life?

⊂⊃

One day, my friend Becca wrote me and said that there might be a common thread, that maybe, over the course of five years, I'd traded one extreme, potentially deadly activity (drinking) for another extreme, potentially deadly activity (climbing). Maybe, Becca suggested, there was a reason for my behavior.

She might be right, I realized. I didn't drink a couple of beers and chill out; I drank as hard as I could as long as I could. I didn't have a cigarette every now and then; I smoked a pack a day, all of them right down to the butt. I didn't take up jogging; I ran a marathon. I dive into everything, and the job gets done, even when it's not a job. When I find a song I like, I play the shit out of it, over and over again, until, after two weeks, I can't listen to it anymore.

Why? What makes me do that? Do I have an "addictive personality"? Is that really a thing? Or is it an excuse? Is it because I grew up in the Midwest, where we finish the job? Is it because my parents instilled a great work ethic in me? Here's what I think: The defining event in my life was getting and staying sober, something that you can't half-ass. If you go at it twenty-three hours a day instead of twenty-four, or fifty-one weeks of the year, you fail. I suppose there was inevitable spillover into the rest of my life. I just put my head down and give it hell, and believe that things will turn out all right.

I left work early one afternoon and paced around the Denver Public Library's journal collection, thumbing through bound archives of the *Journal of Social Psychology*, the *Journal of Experimental Psychology*, and anything else I could find that I thought might contain something of interest.

Finally, I found a study that mentioned a report called *The Course of Alcoholism: Four Years after Treatment*. As an alcoholic four and a half years post-treatment, I wanted to see how I stacked up. What I found was not encouraging: "Many lay groups accept the notion that the disorder is a lifelong disease that may be contained, but never cured. The prevailing view among physicians is similarly pessimistic."

Wow.

I looked at tables of statistics, trying to translate clinical language to figure out what the numbers meant. To me, it looked like just about all of the 548 people studied who had been through treatment decided, at one point over the four-year period after treatment, that it might be okay if they started drinking again. Most didn't binge drink all that often, but they still binge drank. Some fell off the wagon right away; some waited two or three years before doing it.

On page 190: "Only 48 cases (9 percent of the sample) reported abstaining for all 48 months of the period, although many more reported abstaining between 24 and 47 months."

Nine percent. Basically, one in eleven people made it four years. Statistically, everyone I met in treatment was probably drinking again, on some level, and I was the only one still standing. *I'll take those odds*, I thought as I copied the 9 percent sentence into my notebook.

I never questioned the end—I got it; it made sense. I was so messed up the only option was to stop completely. I didn't think everyone needed to do what I did, but the farther I got from it, the less sense drinking made to me. I had no way to self-medicate anymore. The hardest drug I used was caffeine, which isn't the type of thing you binge on at a bachelor party or after you get dumped by your girlfriend. I don't know if I dealt with my emotions in the best way possible, but I never considered that booze would be a better solution. It made me wonder why I even started, why we all start, and not in moderation, especially when we're young.

⸺

High school can be hard on kids, but it wasn't that hard on me. I just had a sad little tug on my heart all the time, a little brick tied around my ankle, pulling me down so my head was just barely bobbing in and out of the water—above it, a cool, confident young man, and below it, a kid wondering why he couldn't exactly sync with anyone else in town.

I spent my adolescence feeling like I didn't fit in. I was on the football team, decent enough to play a fair share, but not good enough to influence the outcome of the game very much. I was smart, but I didn't identify as one of the smart kids. I aced the science portion of the ACT, but the University of Notre Dame rejected me. I missed having the magna cum laude photo on the cover of the local paper by three-thousandths of a grade point.

My senior year, I was finally fast enough to earn a place on the 4 x 100 relay team, but we missed the state track meet by two-tenths of a second. I graduated from high school a virgin. My friends were great, fun guys, but we were just leftovers, who didn't quite fit in with the jocks or the cool party guys.

Drinking cured that, for a few hours a week. I couldn't wait to get to beer number four or five, when I was just like everybody else: I had credibility. I was okay.

I was the least talented of any of my friends when it came to procuring beer, and on the occasions I managed to get some of my own, I couldn't even drink a twelve-pack by myself. This earned me the nickname Single-Digit Leonard.

The summer after I graduated from high school, three things got beer in my hand every weekend: a fake ID, a twenty-seven-year-old coworker, and Saturday morning recycling duty, which allowed me to steal a case of bottled Budweiser from the restaurant a few times.

I got drunk every Friday and Saturday night that summer, wherever the house party was. It was the most incredible summer of my life—the music was great, my friends and I were closer than ever, and I could finally drink twelve beers and remain standing. I didn't even want to leave town for college in August. I was so happy I could have stayed there forever, half-wasted in the summer warmth, music blaring and a few guys and girls around. I had the missing piece. There was no more little tug of sadness. There were no more bad days—just days I was drunk and days I was looking forward to getting drunk.

⊂⊃

Five years sober, I stood in the aisle of Capitol Hill Liquors at Ninth Avenue and Corona Street in Denver, scanning the cooler. *Look at all this fucking beer.* There were so many microbrews since I'd quit drinking, so many different flavors, all these different companies. I couldn't even imagine what all this stuff tasted like. Oatmeal stout, Tripel something something, India pale ale. *Had I ever had an India pale ale?* All those years of guzzling whatever I could to get fucked-up I had never suspected that this would happen. Maybe I could have had a taste of it had I just done things in moderation. I was missing out.

I opened the cooler door. Dale's Pale Ale. Six-pack of cans. It would fit in my backpack for the walk back home. Nick would probably like it. Seemed like it was a pretty popular beer. Ten bucks.

Back at the apartment, I slid the six-pack into the fridge, bottom shelf, right at the front. It was a big deal for me, keeping beer at home, even if it was only for a couple of hours before Nick showed up for dinner. If he drank two beers, I'd send the rest of the six-pack with him when he left. Just a little gesture, flexing my sobriety muscles in the mirror at myself, seeing that they were still there, and maybe a little bigger.

⊂⊃

I had started thinking about climbing all the time, buying guidebooks to areas near Denver, spending late nights researching routes on MountainProject.com, looking at gear, wondering what I should buy next, if I should get more precise shoes, maybe a new rope, or more quickdraws. Obsessing, obsessing, obsessing.

I started going climbing by myself, just bouldering—short, relatively safe routes, sometimes no more than ten feet tall. Above the town of Morrison, just outside Denver, I found one particular section of rock to fixate on.

One day after work, I hiked up the steep hillside above town, my crash pad on my back, looking for that spot in the cliffs. The air was chilly until I got to the base of the wall, where the south-facing rock had been catching winter sun all morning. The face of the cliffs is filled with bouldering problems, sequences of moves up or across the rock face, usually covered with copious amounts of chalk rubbed in by the hands of hundreds of people who have climbed there before.

Bouldering is inherently hard climbing. Most boulder problems don't get more than ten or fifteen feet off the ground, so even though you aren't roped in, the danger from falling is not nearly as high; there are usually more ankle sprains than deaths. The moves are more gymnastic—requiring tiny little holds and awkward stances. The winter I discovered bouldering, I spent too much time on that wall in Morrison, attempting a fifty-foot traverse that never took me more than four or five feet off the ground.

For the first move, I hooked the middle and ring fingers of my right hand into a lip of rock with a hole in the back just big enough for fingertips. I never saw the hole; I had to feel around for it. My left hand was three feet to the left and six inches higher, middle and ring fingers hooked into a two-inch-deep hueco. When I got comfortable, I lifted my right foot up onto a two-inch downward-sloping bump that provided just enough friction to hold about half my body weight. I swung my left heel around the arête, the corner of rock, where, after a couple of tries, I found a little flake that was perfect to hook the rubber heel of my climbing shoe on so I could pull myself around the corner. My butt was about four feet off the ground, and I hugged the rock. If my hands slipped out of the holds, I'd likely flop backward onto a rock that looked like a pirate ship. If I didn't roll back and smash the back of my head, it'd be a miracle.

Fortunately, I had the first move wired by the third try. I pulled myself left with my hooked heel and slid my left hand down onto a hold the size of a thick coffee saucer, then flipped my right hand out of its hole and onto the saucer hold. It was when I slid my feet over and shot my left hand out as far as it could go, desperately searching for a hold in the crack all the way over that I started to panic a little. I was just a stiff breeze away from peeling off the wall, and I almost never hit it on the first try. Still, almost every time I nailed it on the second try, and I stepped over to the crack, where I took a quick deep breath, exhaled, and moved left fast. If I didn't, my forearms would be burning with lactic acid long before the end of the traverse, still forty feet away.

Each time I went to those cliffs, I threw myself into that problem. Every time, I couldn't finish; I got a step closer, though. When I popped off the wall ten or fifteen feet from the end of the traverse, I dropped three feet onto the rocky ground. I cursed the small holds so close to the end that made me crimp both hands into claws. I cursed myself for getting soft from sitting at a desk all day and for not having the fortitude to finish the problem. Then I turned away from the wall and checked the sun, dropping over the shadow of Independence Mountain and Bear Mountain, and I wondered how many tries I'd be able to squeeze in before it got dark.

I had to rest before I tried again, and the more times I tried, the more minutes I had to rest in between tries. My forearms swelled with blood, and I felt like Popeye.

At twenty-eight, I had graduated from pointless shit like sitting on a barstool for hours at a time to pointless shit like crawling sideways across a meaningless rock face and wishing I could just get a few feet farther. It was exactly what I needed.

⌗

I tried to explain climbing to Amy, what I felt up there and why I loved it so much. It must have sounded so foreign, like the things she told me about her graduate courses in the social work program she had enrolled in full-time. I wanted her to try it, just to see if she liked it. Maybe it wouldn't hook her like it had hooked me, but maybe she'd like it enough to join me half the time I went out. She loved hiking and didn't seem to mind backpacking, though she gave up on snowboarding after one lesson, just letting her season pass sit unused. But climbing would be different: I had all the gear, and we didn't have to pay for a lift ticket.

We picked a Saturday. "I'll take you somewhere easy, friendly," I said.

I couldn't believe how small the climbing shoes looked on her feet—the orange Five Ten rock slippers had only four lace holes, compared to the nine on each side of mine. I'd found them on sale on a website and bought them for her, gambling on her interest. She laced them up at the base of the sandstone wall on Grey Rock at Garden of the Gods, the same place Nick and I had taken a climbing lesson the year before and everything had clicked for me.

I scrambled around to the side of the formation and carefully worked my way over to the toprope anchor, ran the rope through a pair of quickdraws clipped into the bolts, and rappeled down.

I tried to be cautiously optimistic. Amy was terrified of heights, something she was quick to point out when I suggested rock climbing. I told her I was too, but that this was a good way to deal with it. Still, I knew it was different for her. The previous year, on the paved path cut into the side of Zion Canyon, she'd all but had a panic attack on the way up to Observation Point. At first diverting her eyes from the drop-off at the edge of the wide trail, she clung to the wall, cowering in fear, as I tried to convince her to take a few more steps. We turned around a mile shy of the viewpoint at the top of the trail. I did my best to hide my disappointment and assure her it was okay.

At the base of the crag in Garden of the Gods, I demonstrated footwork, and we traversed back and forth on small holds and indentations near the bottom of the wall. I explained the system—I'd run the rope up to two bolts at the top, and it would come back down to her, so if she fell, she would only fall a foot or two as the rope gently stretched and caught her.

"Do you want to give it a shot?" I asked. "No pressure. Just go as high as you want, and I'll lower you whenever you say you're ready to come down."

"Okay," she said, tense.

I tied her in, reminding her to concentrate on her feet and breathe. The rock was low-angle at the bottom, becoming a little steeper near the top, but had more features for handholds and footholds.

She stepped onto the slab, cautiously easing her way up.

Be patient. No matter what happened, I was determined not to be like one of those people at the crag who picked a fight with their spouse, one of them hanging thirty or forty feet off the ground and the other holding the rope. All I wanted Amy to do was keep moving upward and eventually get to that anchor sixty feet up, even if it took all day and ten tries.

She moved slowly, not looking down, not shaking, not hyperventilating. She looked almost comfortable—not quite overjoyed, but dealing with the fear and pushing herself. Soon, she was twenty feet off the ground, an achievement in itself. She studied the rock above, and looked at her feet smeared on the wall.

I called up, "Doing great!" for probably the tenth time in as many minutes.

"Okay, I'm good," she said. "I'm ready to come down."

"Are you sure?" I said. "You can lean back on the rope and hang right there, and then start up again when you're ready." *Baby steps*, I reminded myself.

"Nope, I'm good," she said. "I'll come down."

"Okay," I said. "Nice job. Just gently lean back and put your weight on the rope." I pulled in all the slack and slowly let rope through the belay device as she began to inch down the wall toward me.

⸻

By the end of our climbing date, she had made it to the top of the route, slapping the anchor and letting me take a couple of photos before she came down. It was huge, all-time, in the history of good sports in relationships.

But she didn't love it, and I knew it. She did it once, for me, not because she wanted to do it. She survived the climb all the way to the top, and a while later, when I asked if she wanted to do another lap, she declined.

I guess I still thought of climbing as some sort of hobby, just a thing I did but Amy and I didn't do together—although I would have loved it if we could have. I don't know if, at the time, either of us thought it was a sign that we shouldn't be together anymore.

⸺

With six months to plan, we had decided to get married in June—not a big traditional ceremony, just a small family-and-friends event in Zion National Park. She didn't even want to wear a white dress.

It made sense: We had been together for eight years, on and off, but had been happy living together the past three years. I was twenty-eight, she was twenty-nine, and if we were married, she could get on my health insurance. There was no engagement ring (she'd said she didn't want one), no big proposal, just a few conversations in the kitchen that led to, "Well, let's get married then. Where should we do it?"

In the months leading up to the wedding, my mom pressured me almost weekly to cut my increasingly unruly ponytail-length hair. When maintained, I had Shirley Temple curls, but usually my hair was a big collection of tangled split ends poking out under my bicycle helmet. My mom really wanted me to look nice for the wedding, she said. Then she said it again the next week, and the next.

"What if we gave you some money?" she asked.

"Mom," I said. "I can afford a haircut."

Then the offer came via my dad.

"Your mom wants to give you some money to get a haircut," Dad said one Sunday a couple of weeks before the big day.

I laughed. It had come to this. "Like how much money?" I asked Dad.

"Five hundred bucks," he said.

"Holy shit," I laughed. "She really means it."

"I'll throw in some too," he said, not laughing but not dead serious either. "Two hundred bucks, plus a little money to pay for the haircut."

"I think we might have a deal," I said.

We weren't throwing an extravagant party and asking our parents to pay for a venue, a DJ or a band, an open bar, or any of that stuff. Seven hundred bucks would be enough money to buy some climbing gear—a handful of cams and chocks, enough to get me started up some longer traditionally protected routes. It probably seemed like a good investment to Mom and Dad, since they figured you only get married once. At the time I thought that too.

<hr>

We went to Zion, said our vows underneath the sandstone peak of the Watchman, welcomed all our friends to this special place in the desert, and drove back to Denver, back to Amy's studies and my mountains.

With my parents' haircut money, I bought myself a wedding present, just for me: eight cams, a set of wired stoppers, and a bunch of shoulder-length slings—the beginning of my trad rack.

Shortly after the wedding, my friend Lee talked me into my first alpine climb. "I've been looking at the north ridge of Mount Toll for years," Lee said. "It's only 5.6, three pitches, up in the Indian Peaks."

I said yes instantly, excited to actually climb actual mountains. *Holy shit.*

Lee, a forty-eight-year-old aircraft mechanic with decades of climbing experience, had become my mentor in trad climbing. He took me up the multipitch rock routes near Denver, showing me how to place cams and chocks, how to climb cracks, and how to build anchors at belays. We liked each other's bad jokes, and when he needed a partner, I always happened to be available. On Mount Toll, I'd only have to follow him up the three hundred feet of technical climbing just below the summit, belay, and listen.

<hr>

Midway through the third pitch of climbing, I thought to myself what a hero I looked like, deftly picking handholds and footholds, climbing up the side of that mountain with an ice ax strapped to my pack (an ice ax!), roped up to my partner perched eighty feet above me on a ledge, with nothing but air around us, the granite-and-snow waves of the Indian Peaks as a backdrop.

I followed the pitch easily, removing all the gear Lee had placed on his way up, and we packed up the rope and started traversing south across the west face of the peak to head for the summit. It wasn't my first time in the big hills; I knew enough to step carefully and check every rock I put my hands on. A slip on a loose stone or a handhold breaking could send me tumbling a steep fourteen hundred feet off the Continental Divide to the talus slope above Pawnee Lake. When they retrieved my body, it would be lucky if my head was still attached.

I moved slowly, carefully. When I got to a rock about the size of a pillow at about 12,800 feet, I prepared to step around it, my back to the void. I gave it a little tug, assuming it would hold.

At that elevation, it's a little harder for your brain to get oxygen, because there's about 40 percent less of it in the air than at sea level. You have to take in almost two breaths to get the same amount of oxygen you'd normally get from a single breath if you were standing in, say, the Merle Hay Mall in Des Moines. Your heart works a lot harder up high, sometimes so hard you can hear your neck pulsing. The upside is, when you scare the shit out of yourself by doing something that could kill you, your heart jumping into your throat feels pretty much normal.

As I sidestepped to the right, the rock I hung onto ground out a rock-on-rock groan and started to slide, ready to take me for the ride of my life. My stomach leapt upward as the rock slid down onto my bare ankle and my climbing-shoe-encased foot, and it stopped.

I didn't scream, I didn't pee my pants, and I didn't barrel down the side of Mount Toll into Pawnee Lake. I stood, just like that, with the rock sitting on my foot, both hands on it, and I took a couple of breaths.

Lee had turned around. "You're not hurt, are you?" he asked.

"No, I'm fine," I said, looking at the rock like it was an old television I had dropped while walking up a flight of stairs. "I'm just trying to figure out how to get this thing off my foot without falling off."

If I pulled my foot out from underneath it and couldn't get out of the way when the rock rolled, it would take me down the mountainside with it. I maneuvered my body as far to the right as possible, then pushed the rock up slightly. I gingerly pulled my left foot out from underneath it, then lowered the rock an inch to rest, however tenuously.

Out of the way, I pulled my hands off it, expecting it to thunder away in a quick exit. Nothing. It just sat there, content. It had sat on top of that mountain for a million years before I disturbed it, and now it was going to sit for a million more in its new spot.

Okay okay okay. Exhale.

I picked my way up the final one hundred feet to the summit at great-grandmother speed. At the top, we switched out our climbing shoes for boots. Two minutes before we started down, it started to sleet and thunder. I secretly beamed at the adventure my life had become.

⸺

A month and a half later, I stood in the parking lot of the Safeway in Seward, Alaska, snapping photos while Amy munched a bowl of granola on the tailgate of the car. The lush green slopes and sharp northeast ridge of Mount Marathon towered over the store, climbing a steep forty-six hundred feet from sea level in two lateral miles. In the other direction, a fence of glaciated peaks lined the east shore of deep-blue Resurrection Bay.

We were at the midpoint of our honeymoon, living out of a rented Dodge Caliber station wagon that happened to be just long enough for us to sleep in the back every night. At the city campground, instead of pitching a tent in in one of the sites far back from the bay, we paid for an RV spot and backed the car up to the shore in between forty-foot motor homes, taking in the view of the water and the mountains through the open hatchback.

I was in heaven, living cheaply out of a car, sleeping in the back, driving and hiking all over the southern part of Alaska. We'd seen Denali from the highway, rising 17,000 feet above the road, so tall and huge you thought it was a cloud at first. We had backpacked into a backcountry cabin on Crow Pass and been visited by mountain goats, kayaked in Resurrection Bay, and hiked up to look at the enormous Harding Icefield. The car, a place to sleep safe from Alaska's legendary grizzly bears, had kept Amy happy. Until our last night of sleeping out before the end of our trip.

At a campground south of Anchorage, I pitched our MSR tent, which four of my friends had bought us as a wedding gift—and the only item on the registry I'd been excited about.

After we ate dinner, Amy said she'd rather sleep in the car.

"But it's a nice night," I said, "and it doesn't even look like it's going to rain." Plus, I'd already put the tent up.

"I would just rather sleep in the car tonight," she said.

"Why?" I asked.

"Bears," she said.

"I think we'll be okay as long as we don't bring food in the tent with us," I said. "Bear attacks are rare. And attacks on people sleeping in a tent are even rarer." Plus, we were really close to civilization, a couple hundred feet from the highway. Plus, we had bear spray. "You slept in the tent for two nights at the campground in Denali National Park, and we were fine, weren't we?"

I didn't let it go, didn't say, "Okay, I'll just sleep in the car with you." We didn't argue or get mad. I just went to sleep in the tent by myself while my wife slept in the car thirty feet away.

In the morning, it was a little weird, but we both let it go and wrapped up the trip—me in love with Alaska, feeling like I'd just scratched the surface. Alaska was a dream come true for me, maybe the jumping-off point for other things, bigger things.

Maybe I should have seen it, an obvious sign of something bigger, that I was falling in love with one vision of life and Amy was falling in love with another one. I was enamored with road trips, living out of a car, climbing, exploring, getting dirty, drinking morning coffee in a puffy jacket, and looking down at dirty toes poking out of my sandals. She wanted a backyard, a garden, and a dog.

Back in Denver that fall, at a happy hour event I had to attend as part of my newspaper job, I met a guy and his wife from Iowa, and the guy told me he'd had three drunk-driving arrests but that he quit drinking for three years, and now he has three kids. He was sitting next to me, drinking his second beer of the night.

We were in a restaurant that had about a hundred beers on tap, and I instantaneously, genuinely wondered:

if I am making a big deal out of this whole "alcoholism" thing
and
if maybe I'm taking it too seriously
and
if I should order a beer.

Just take it in moderation—one or two, that's all. Just to loosen up. No big deal. No big deal.

I was five and a half years sober.

Maybe five and a half years is enough. Just to loosen up. No big deal. Actually taste the beer this time around, enjoy it, not guzzle it to get drunk. Can I do that? I probably can, right? This guy had three DUIs. Three. Hell, I only had two. And it's not like I killed someone.

Just one, to loosen up.

What goes well with these nachos? Microbrew? Stout? IPA? No big deal. Whatever he's drinking looks good. Amber something or other. He's got kids, and he's drinking here, on a weeknight, with his wife. How bad can it be?

I am not listening to what you are saying right now. I am thinking about a beer.

Just one? Of course not. I can't do things half-assed—especially that. I cannot live the life I've found and have a few beers here and there.

I am a climber and a writer and a dreamer, and already there isn't time enough for all of it. There are mountains and sunsets, miles of trails and rivers, grizzly bears and marmots. Smiles and heartbreak, and love and loss and pain. I want to take it all head-on, to go for that next handhold, even when I don't know if I'm going to stick the move or take a wicked screamer down the face of the rock.

My life wasn't in here, sitting on my ass with this guy. It was out there, thanks to sixty meters of climbing rope, with my heavy pack and all the heart and courage I could dig up. It smells like that rope and pine trees and sunbaked skin, and it fits like a finger lock in a centimeter-wide seam in perfect granite. It's in my dad's smile when he gets a photo of me standing somewhere in our beloved Rocky Mountains, with the sun low on my tired but happy face, after another long day of running out my demons. It comes out in hour-long bursts of longhand, frantically inked in all capitals in a beat-up composition book. And when it's good, really good, it puts a lump in my throat.

I wasn't going to miss out on any of it, no matter how low or how high it got, just because, what, I wanted to remember what good beer tasted like, or how it made me feel? I'd have missed a life.

I picked up the glass of water in front of me and drank the rest before politely excusing myself and pedaling my bike through the dark streets of downtown Denver as fast as I could, weaving in and out of traffic, dodging potholes, not touching my brake levers.

CLOSURE

HALFWAY UP THE THIRD FLATIRON, the iconic twelve-hundred-foot rock tower above Boulder, Colorado, I started thinking that I could definitely slip and fall. If I fell from that height, I would certainly die, and everyone would think I did it on purpose, because I had just filed my divorce papers sixteen hours before and I'd climbed up here without a rope.

But everyone would have been mistaken. I was up here, hanging onto this red-brown sandstone, because I needed to clear my head. I had the week off work, and I couldn't sit in my tiny postsplit apartment all day. That would have been unhealthy.

Of course, this could turn out to be really unhealthy. I looked down at my feet, clad in my tiny sticky-rubber-soled climbing shoes. *As long as they stick to this rock for another hundred moves or so, I should be just fine. Then I can get back onto flat ground and back to feeling like someone punched me in the stomach.*

⸺

Amy and I had been together for almost nine years, through all my problems, and hers. Through Christmases and rehab and jail and counseling. When we'd met at a bar when we were in college, I was already an alcoholic, and she was an anorexic/bulimic sorority girl.

Since then, we had changed. She'd lived in Omaha and western New York, and I'd lived in Idaho and Montana. We got back together in Phoenix and then moved to Denver. She was a makeup artist before deciding on a career in social work. I worked at small newspapers before landing at a nonprofit that took inner-city kids on backpacking trips.

I wanted to climb, to get out there and see it all—snow-covered peaks, rivers that cut canyons, the moonscape of the American desert—to bring it into myself and see what it made me. When I asked Amy to go hiking and she said she had to stay home and study, I went climbing instead. Each conversation we had, I lost more hope for our marriage and got closer and closer to calling it dead. She studied her new passion, and I had the best climbing year of my life, attacking routes with a sad and angry ferocity that pushed past my normal fear.

We moved out of the apartment we had shared for two and a half years, the longest I had lived anywhere since I had left my parents' house in Iowa. I broke down going through my things, not knowing what to do with photos of the two of us having a great time, photos from our wedding, gifts she had given me, notes she had written, things that you save when it's forever and don't have a box for when it's suddenly not.

⸺

A backpacking trip with five at-risk teens from East Palo Alto, California, already scheduled for the days right after we moved out of our apartment, had turned out to be the perfect solace for me. It took me into the mountains south of Yosemite and forced me to slow down.

I was eager to introduce these city kids to mountain sunsets, real silence, and big peaks, and talk to them about their lives, which were infinitely tougher at seventeen than mine was at twenty-nine. I had to focus on getting them through their first-ever week in the wilderness, where they were living out of a backpack, drinking alpine lake water, and crapping in holes in the ground. I had to forget about my divorcé studio apartment, where I didn't have a blender or a toaster or a space in bed next to someone who believed in me.

In the mornings before anyone else woke up, I sat and took photos of Chittenden Lake, so placid and flat just after sunup that it held a perfect reflection of the granite slabs and skinny pines around it. For those few minutes, the tension in my shoulders eased, and I felt the tiniest bit of calm. When things are good, that view and that quiet don't melt into you as deeply.

I had asked Amy to pick me up at the Denver airport at the end of my trip, since we were going to try to remain friends and she had the afternoon off. We had agreed to file the divorce papers after I got back from California.

At 2:40 p.m., I got in her car and she said we needed to hurry because the city clerk's office closed at four. She'd filled out all the forms for the divorce and put them in a yellow folder in the backseat. I tried to make sense of them as Amy drove.

At 3:20, we were still a mile from the City and County Building in downtown Denver. I asked Amy if she had brought a checkbook, knowing we needed to pay $200 in fees. Shit, no, neither of us had. We drove to my apartment building, I ran up the stairs to my still-not-lived-in apartment, and ripped out a blank check. We parked as close as we could and hurried through the building to room 280A, getting there at exactly 3:40.

⸺

We had failed, fucked it up, gotten all those people together for our wedding. We had stood there in front of everyone and said it was forever, that we loved each other. And we blew it. I hated myself, even though Amy had told me it wasn't anyone's fault, that people change, people grow apart. When she'd said that, worse than crying, I instead felt sick to just below the point of tears, like someone was sitting on my chest when I tried to get out of bed.

Amy had never liked climbing, which I realized now was a perfectly normal thing. We've spent thousands of years devising systems to avoid risk and maximize safety and comfort; it seems pretty natural to not try climbing up something from which you could very easily fall to your death.

But climbing worked for me. The nuances of holding onto rock features with only the friction and balance of toes and fingertips, the crucial placement of safety equipment every few moves, keeping the rope at the right tension—all these things demanded full attention, forcing me to leave my problems on the ground. Climbing taught me to persevere through debilitating fear, when I hyperventilated and was so overcome with the likelihood of falling that both legs shook hard enough to jackhammer themselves right off the tiny footholds, but I kept it together and kept going.

That kind of simplicity was appealing when I sat in my apartment on the one chair I'd kept in the split. I was sure I'd just made the biggest decision of my young life, but not sure it was the right one.

The morning after we filed the divorce papers, I woke up early, not hungry; I was too nervous to eat. I stuffed a small backpack with everything I needed: a harness, a belay device, a chalk bag, climbing shoes, a light static rope—usable only for rappeling, unsafe to use for climbing. No climbing partner. No helmet—a helmet wasn't going to do anything for me if I fell this time. This was going to be my first ropeless climb.

I had climbed the Third Flatiron twice before, roped. It was easy, low-angle, like a thousand-foot ladder into the sky. It wasn't much of a challenge for many climbers in Boulder—they would leave from the Chautauqua Park trailhead, run to the base of the climb, slip on their climbing shoes, and race up the face, rappeling off the back and returning to the car in less than an hour.

For me, though, this time was serious. No matter how easy the climb, it could still kill you. One move, upsetting your balance, one foot slipping, one hand greasing off a hold, and you're rag-dolling down the rock.

⸺

I walked quickly up the trail from Chautauqua Park, breaking a light sweat in the warm early fall air. Near the base of the rock, the trail steepened, and I wove up the switchbacks, arriving at the East Bench in just under forty minutes. I popped off my hiking shoes, pulled my climbing shoes out of my pack, slipped them on, and tried to focus.

I thought about my friend Bruce, who had once, wrestling with a heavy life decision, made it all the way up to the top of the wall at a climbing gym before noticing he had never clipped himself into a belay line. Trying to traverse across the plastic wall to a safe spot, he slipped and fell thirty feet. He was in the trauma unit of the hospital for five days with a collapsed lung, broken ribs, and a broken elbow.

I sat there at the base of the climb, the *Standard East Face*, and tried to get my shit together. I stood up on one foot, pulling my other foot up and resting it against the inside of my knee, brought my hands together and pointed them above my head, a yoga tree pose. *This will quiet things down.* I focused, kept my balance for ten breaths, then switched to the other foot.

I looked up at one thousand feet of sandstone and took a deep breath.

Boy, if I fall off this thing, no one will know that this morning is the lowest I've ever felt in my life since that first year after I stopped drinking.

Deep breath.

Was the divorce all my fault? All the damage from my drinking, too?

Deep breath.

Take it easy. It's not that simple.

And there I was, looking up at this gigantic rock, a giant sandstone skyscraper tilted into a mountain.

The answer is up there.

It wasn't like I expected to get a message from someone at the top or have an epiphany about the course of my life—but maybe the answer was in the process.

I had come here to pull myself up this rock, to interact with it, and to think about nothing else besides what I need to do to keep moving up and not fall. I moved up, running a filmstrip of what happened yesterday in the back of my head.

———

Back in 5 Minutes, a sign taped to the door at 280A had said. But almost immediately, a woman came out of the office across the hall and let us in. We sat down at a desk with her and watched her go through our forms. *Are we really killing this?*

Another woman stuck her head through the door and said, "Can I ask you a question?"

The woman looking at our forms said, "Yes, come on in and have a seat."

No privacy for us.

The woman with our paperwork asked, "Do you have any assets? Children? And there isn't a pregnancy?"

She labeled a couple of the forms and explained that we needed to take them across the hall to the Office of the Clerk and Recorder and have a notary watch us sign them. We'd already screwed up and signed one of them before she told us this.

As we walked into the hallway to look for the notary, Amy started to get choked up.

"Are you okay?" I said. "Are you going to be okay?" *I still care about you, you know. I don't want you to be sad while we're filing our divorce papers.* I was dizzy.

"Yeah," Amy said. "I'm okay." But the way she said it I knew she was two breaths away from a sob.

My throat was in a knot. *Why couldn't I make this right?*

On the forms, we'd had to write the city where we got married. Springdale, Utah, it said in Amy's handwriting. I remembered the excitement of our wedding, and the couple of days leading up to it, and—

Stop.

Amy swallowed.

At the notary counter, the woman said to make the check out for $220, and that we needed to make copies of all the forms on the copy machine behind us. A bike messenger was in line behind us, but the notary wouldn't wait on him until she was done with us. He sighed. Amy ripped the staples out, saying it would be faster if we sent everything through at once.

I started to argue, but then stopped myself. *Jesus Christ, can we just get through this, the last thing we ever do together?* We had rarely fought until six months ago.

We sent the stack of pages through, restapled them, and turned around and gave them to the notary. We watched her stamp everything.

I was sure I heard the bike messenger say, "You gotta be kidding me." I was ready to shove him through the glass door.

On the happiest day of your life, you get a best man and as many groomsmen as you want. She gets a maid of honor and a bunch of pretty bridesmaids. That's the beginning. But when it ends, you get this hollow government hall and this fucking asshole bike messenger. I gritted my teeth.

Amy and I ended up sitting next to each other on a bench in Cheesman Park, crying and talking about how much we still cared. I didn't care if all the joggers and cyclists in the park saw tears rolling down my face; I couldn't stop it.

I hugged her good-bye in front of my apartment, and she said she'd call when she was ready to talk again. The door had closed on our relationship. It was the first time in nine years that the door would be all the way shut.

Now, at the base of the Third Flatiron, eight hundred feet of sandstone above my head, I chalked up. I stepped one foot onto the stone, smearing a stance, grabbing a handhold, then the next one. *Pay attention.* I moved left out onto the enormous east face, as wide as a football field. I traversed, and the exposure opened up underneath me. I pictured myself falling, rolling into a bag of blood and broken bones onto the talus below. I stepped up, keeping three points of contact at all times.

Only a few people I knew would make sense of what I was doing. I was out here climbing on my own to take me away. In bed the night before, unable to sleep, I'd thought about going somewhere for a drink. A bar for a few beers. Hell, a park bench and a bottle of cheap red wine. Whatever. Six and a half years of sobriety, gone. The crushing feeling of failure, gone, too. It was just for a second, for a flash, that I'd considered it a serious option. Then it had disappeared.

In twenty minutes, I was halfway up the face, out of breath. I stopped to rest, looking behind me for the first time. I was slowly leaving Boulder on the ground, with all my problems.

I turned, kept climbing, and then I stopped. I was in a strange spot, where the handholds are far apart, and I'd have to step high to grab the next one, leaving only one foot and a few fingers on the rock. I started to go for it, and then I slowly lowered myself back down. This wasn't the time to take risks. I made two moves to the right, then up, then back left to my line. All secure moves.

And just like that, I was on top of the Third. The first time I climbed this, with Nick, it had taken us hours to get to this spot. I pulled my skinny rope out of my pack, put on my harness, zipped down the west face, and was on the ground.

On the walk back to the car, I realized I didn't really enjoy climbing by myself. It was too risky, and there was no one to share the views with, talk about the moves, the rock, life. It was my first ropeless solo climb ever, but maybe my last as well.

⸺

I had gone to a few appointments with a therapist when Amy and I were deciding whether to get divorced, and my therapist had recommended I do some sort of ritual to give closure to our relationship—burning some clothes, cutting off my hair, something like that. I looked back up at the Third, towering above Chautauqua Park, wondering if I'd really gotten closure up there. I still felt terrible, and I would for over a year. But when it got tough, I looked to the mountains for answers instead of in a bottle. That was a different type of closure.

That was the day I started to try to forget all my memories with a person I loved. The day I started to adjust to a new part of my life, the part when I'm not in love anymore, the part where I'm alone.

The afternoon after I climbed the Third, my parents arrived from Iowa for a three-day weekend. My mom said I looked thin, and I think we both knew it was the type of thing that comes when you are so heartbroken you don't think about food often enough. My hair was chopped down to a half inch, making me look even thinner.

"You don't have a TV?" Mom asked, looking around my tiny four-hundred-square-foot studio on Marion Street the next morning.

"Nah, Amy kept ours," I said. "It's okay. I don't feel like I need one."

"We can buy you one," she said. Dad nodded.

"I can afford a TV, Mom. I just don't feel like I need one." I had been in the studio four weeks, and although it was small and I was sad, I didn't think the apartment was sad. The east wall was all windows, so there was lots of sunshine in the morning. I had a small desk—the kitchen table from my apartment with Amy—a bed, and a place for my bicycle. There was a small storage unit in the basement for my skis and backpacks.

I suppose it didn't feel like much of a home to my mom, who hadn't lived in an apartment in thirtysome years, let alone a tiny one. I finished toweling off the breakfast dishes while my parents sipped coffee on the stools next to the kitchen counter.

"Should we head up to Boulder Canyon then?" I said.

I drove Mom's sedan up the winding canyon road to the parking area across from the Boulderado, a short low-angle granite slab on the north side of the canyon. My friend Lee jokingly called the crag "the fierce Boulderado," but I loved taking people there. It had four really beginner-friendly routes, a 5.4, two 5.5s, and a 5.6, all with toprope bolts.

I shouldered a pack and looked up canyon and down canyon. When traffic was clear, I led Mom and Dad across the road.

"Be careful on this trail," I said, turning around to Mom as she walked right behind me. "It's pretty loose."

The Boulderado had one of the easiest approaches in Colorado, maybe sixty seconds of walking and scrambling from the parking area across the street, a blip that I could probably negotiate with my eyes closed at this point. I had spent hours and hours in the mountains doing scrambling like that. But Mom and Dad were getting older. Sometime while living out West, I had crossed the threshold where you start looking to take care of your parents instead of them taking care of you.

They waited on the wide ledge twenty feet above the road as I went up to the back of the formation, climbing down and setting up a toprope on the anchors above the easiest route. I rappeled down the ropes and, out of the corner of my eye, saw Dad take a photo of me.

Dad was just along to watch, but Mom wanted to try climbing. She put on the climbing shoes I had bought for her, and I took her around to some low-angle slabs at the base of the crag to show her how the rubber would stick to even the smallest feature. I told her to keep her butt out away from the rock to ensure maximum friction on the low-angle slabs. "Remember to use your feet, not your hands, Mom," I said. "You can stand for a long time on two tiny footholds, but you can't hang your entire body weight on your hands for very long."

She was fifty-nine, five foot two, maybe 110 pounds, and had started bruising easily the last few years. I certainly had no illusions about her hanging from one hand Sylvester Stallone–style. I just wanted her to have fun, and understand what I did in the mountains every weekend, if just a little bit.

I gave her my extra helmet, helped her into my extra harness, doubling back all the buckles, and tied her into the rope.

"Okay, Mom, if you get tired, scared, or your hands won't hang on anymore, remember, you can come off the rock and just sit on the rope," I said. "I'll keep the belay tight, so you won't fall more than a foot, and the rope will stretch a tiny bit and catch your weight. You ready?"

My mom was a lifelong flatlander, her blue eyes—the ones she had given me—matched the blue plastic of the helmet. She said, "Yep!" and started up her first rock climb.

When had this happened before, but in reverse? A swimming pool twenty-five years ago, a roller coaster in Kansas City, a tennis court in southwest Iowa, on a plastic sled somewhere at the top of a hill when I was three feet tall and covered in so many layers I looked like the Michelin Man.

Mom was not the smoothest, most natural-looking first-time rock climber. Probably like I did on my first climb, she reached in jerky movements, feeling the rock with her feet instead of looking for features and then carefully placing her toes. She was not a natural athlete, but neither was I. Mom could walk you into the ground, though. And she ran for years and years. Friends always told me, "I saw your mom out running today"—in the rain, in the snow, whatever. She finally gave it up after her knees started hurting too much. But then she just went for walks, flying up and down hills at four miles per hour.

We lived at the top of a big hill in a town in southwest Iowa until I was fourteen, and Mom would ride her bike back from the tennis courts with me as I battled my bike up the hill. We never got off and pushed; I just stood up in the pedals of my heavy black-and-gold Huffy Thunder 50 BMX bike, legs burning, until we got to an intersection about halfway up the hill. Instead of stopping, she'd tell me just to ride in circles until my legs felt better and I could go on. Two decades later when I became a mountain climber, I walked up trails and talus fields until my legs and lungs were on fire, and I just kept going, grinding it out until there was no more mountain to climb—just like my mom taught me.

On the Boulderado, Mom found the holds in the granite, working her way up, around the tree a third of the way up, into the dihedral, around the bulge to the anchors. She didn't get pumped, didn't tremble once, didn't ask to come down. She kept going until she stood up on the big ledge at the top.

"Mom, you have to touch the anchor," I yelled. "Reach up and slap it." She did. I laughed.

"Okay, I'm going to take in the slack," I yelled up. "When you're ready, pull your hands off the rock and lean back on the rope."

She took a quick look around the top of the fierce Boulderado and leaned back. I slowly let out slack and talked her down the route until her feet were on the ledge next to mine and Dad's. She turned to us with a huge smile.

Maybe it was watching Mom float up the climb so easily, or just curiosity, but I said, "Dad, what do you think? Want to give it a try?" I fully expected him to brush it off.

"Yeah," he said. "I think I can give it a try."

He tried on all three pairs of my climbing shoes, squeezing into the purple Five Ten Spires. I helped him into the harness and tied a figure eight, Mom gave him the helmet, and he was off. He moved quickly up the granite, maybe remembering all the scrambling he'd done in Colorado when he lived in Poudre Park, a few canyons north, for a few months thirty-plus years ago. At the top, he tapped the bolts with one hand, and I yelled up the same instructions I'd told Mom.

He stepped to the edge of the big ledge, tried to lean back, then started to downclimb, then back up to the ledge, then started to downclimb the blocky gully to the right of the anchors, where he'd gone up. Once in the gully, he stepped down to a comfortable spot, where he tried to let me lower him again. But he couldn't quite put all of his weight, and trust, in the rope that ran through the anchor above his head.

"Okay, Dad, you just have to trust the rope," I yelled up, pulling in all the slack. "It'll work. You just have to commit to it."

He spent maybe five minutes in that gully—leaning back a little, trying to let both hands off the rock, resituating himself, never quite comfortable. Finally, he leaned back and gingerly sat into the harness, watching the rope take his weight, and I let an inch of rope through my belay device, then another one.

"Put your hands on the rope, Dad, and put your feet out in front of you and just walk down," I said. "I got you. I got you. Gonna let you down really slow. Relax. I got you."

He stepped onto the ledge next to Mom and me as I let out the last of the rope.

"I guess that was some sort of metaphor about trusting your son, huh?" I joked. "I gotta tell you, Dad, I understand your hesitation."

We all laughed.

—

The next day, back in Denver, my parents drove me to the Best Buy on Colorado Boulevard and refused to leave the store until I picked out a TV. I got a small one, the size of a computer monitor, with a DVD player built in, and they were happy.

CAN'T

I DIPPED MY HAND INTO MY chalk bag for the fifth time in thirty seconds, and I heard the first of the two voices I hear regularly in my head. One is instinctual, looking out for my safety. It speaks up when I'm climbing. Sometimes it's hard to hear anything over it, especially in a place like the first twenty-five feet of a route called Pear Buttress on Lumpy Ridge, near Estes Park, Colorado. The start of the route is what's called "unprotected," meaning if you fall, you deck; you slide down the granite and slam into slabs of rock that used to be part of the face above. This means whatever part of you hits first is probably going to break. Hopefully just your ankles, but it all depends on how you fall.

It was February when my coworker Chris and I took the day off work to try to climb Pear Buttress. Early in the week the weather forecast had made it seem possible—sunny and high of forty-seven. But by the time we were driving up to Estes Park, it had changed to partly cloudy and high of forty-three. Chris and I shared a desk at the nonprofit where we worked in Denver, and we had started to get out together more and more often to climb on the weekends. Everything about Chris was efficient and trim: his black hair always cropped to a quarter inch, his backpack tiny for whatever objective, the rack a little smaller than I'd like. He was comfortable pushing himself, and he pushed me to climb harder routes than I might have with other people.

At the base of Pear Buttress, I had a few hundred dollars' worth of protective equipment clipped to my harness—a couple dozen carabiners, fifteen cams, and a set of wired stoppers. I was securely tied in, and Chris was belaying me. Yet all of this meant nothing until I could get myself to make a very delicate traverse across a blank slab into the security of a two-inch-wide crack that runs up the next thirty feet. I stood, hanging from the toes of my climbing shoes, on two nubs of rock invisible from the ground, fingers of my right hand clutching the only good handhold on the face.

To make the next move, you have to let go of this hold. That's when I heard the first voice.

You can't do it. That's all it said.

That's all the voice had to say, because I knew I couldn't do it. I didn't have the courage, balls, skill, technique, the will, whatever. I was just a kid from Iowa who never should have left.

What am I doing up here? Trying to prove something? I'm going to fall off this rock and hit the ground so fast Chris won't be able to do anything but maybe drop the rope to frantically run underneath me and try to break my fall.

I heard the voice again. *You can't do it.*

I looked down. It was twenty-five feet, easily. I'd be scared to jump into a swimming pool off a diving board that high. *Fuck this. I'm climbing down.*

But when I looked down at the line I had climbed, I realized I had pulled my way up almost completely on friction footwork.

Where are the holds? How did I climb up that?

Trying to climb down would be suicide. I wasn't even sure I could backtrack to the last tiny foothold I had used.

You can't do it.

There were three options from where I stood: stand where I was until my feet became too fatigued to hold my toes at this angle and I slipped and fell to the ground; foolishly try to climb backward, again risking a fall, albeit hopefully a slightly shorter fall; or try to climb into the crack to my left.

To get to the crack, I would have to take my left toes off a thin smear, spread-eagle my legs, reach my toes out onto the flake of rock four feet to my left, and hope the rubber on my shoe stuck. If my foot slipped, I would likely cartwheel off the rock and land headfirst at Chris's feet, like a lawn dart.

You can't do it.

Fuck it. I'm doing it. I'm doing it. I'm doing it I'm doing it I'm doing it.

I pointed my left shoe toward the flake and slowly, slowly reached my foot out. My toes stuck. I quickly jammed a hand in the crack, pulled a cam off my harness, and plugged it into the rock, then hastily clipped the rope to it, hyperventilating. Now if I fell, I wouldn't hit the ground.

When Mark, my counselor at the Horizons treatment program, told me that I couldn't white-knuckle my way through sobriety, I'm sure this was not what he had in mind.

A couple more hand jams and I stepped out onto the face. I did it. I had finished the most terrifying fifteen minutes of rock climbing I'd done in my life, standing on a two-foot-wide ledge a hundred feet off the ground.

⸺

I hear the voice when I'm not climbing, too. It says the same thing, but it wants to wreck my life. It speaks out more often—sometimes daily.

One morning at work, I got an email that contained the innocent phrase "pitcher of beer." For some reason, that day, my mind latched onto that phrase, instead of skimming over it for whatever else was in the email, and I immediately visualized a pitcher of beer.

I saw a pitcher of golden American beer, Budweiser probably, with a one-inch foam head on top, and I could smell it that day, taste it—bitter, cool, musty. There were four pint glasses' worth of beer in the pitcher, and I could get to the bottom of it in a few minutes, I was sure. I knew how heavy it was, and I could feel myself sitting up to lift it with both hands to my mouth, sticking my nose in the foam.

You can't do it, the voice said. *You can't avoid beer. Not for the rest of your life. Maybe not even for the rest of this week.*

More importantly, you don't have to do it. You don't owe anybody shit. You're an adult. You can make your own decisions. Have a beer, like a normal person. Like a man. Hell, have ten. You deserve it.

And I knew if I did, the taste would feel like going home, better than going home.

⸺

It would be easy to say "Look at you—you used to drink a lot, and now you're a climber. You're just substituting one rush for another."

I don't think that's it though. For me, climbing was about learning a different way to deal with the world, and the challenges of life. It's no more heroic to spend your weekend hours climbing up some pointless rock face, risking death and injury, just "because it's there," or whatever, than it is to sit in a bar and get drunk all weekend. But it certainly takes a little more ambition.

I'm not an exceptional climber. Although I've kept myself alive and my name out of the Monday morning "Climber Rescued" headlines in the *Denver Post* and Boulder's *Daily Camera*, I haven't stood on top of the world's biggest peaks or climbed anything close to the most difficult lines.

But I do consider myself an exceptional recovering addict. I can deal with the challenges of addiction because of what I've learned in the mountains—perseverance, balance, endurance, patience, accountability.

Alpinist and writer Kelly Cordes once said, "One of the cool things about alpinism is that you end up being responsible for your own decisions, which doesn't happen in today's world hardly at all anymore. There's always someone else to blame. But you go climbing, it's usually you're the one to blame, as to whether you get up or down, mixed in with some luck . . . Nobody ever guaranteed any of us anything."

I see parallels in the personal responsibility of climbing and the personal responsibility of recovery. Relapsing, to me, is not an option, and if it happened, I'd have no one to blame but myself. At some point, every relapsing addict makes a conscious choice to give up and walk into a liquor store, or call someone who can get them meth, or steal their mother's painkiller prescription. I sometimes imagined finding the words to tell my mom and dad that I'd relapsed, and I could never figure out anything that would sound like a real reason, besides "I gave up on myself."

After almost seven years of sobriety, it wasn't just a number of sober calendar days I would lose, it was a whole belief system that would crash down. I figure if I'm tough enough to stay sober, I'm tough enough for anything. And if I'm suddenly not tough enough to stay sober, then what? In addiction, just like climbing, you can't fall off if you don't let go.

⸺

Six months after I'd taken my mom on her first-ever rock climb, in Colorado, she decided she was going to check out her local climbing gym, completely on her own, with no suggestion or hint from me.

"Kathy Stubbs and I are going to Climb Iowa next Saturday to take the belay class," she said at the other end of the line during our weekly Sunday phone call.

During my Christmas visit home a couple of months before, my brother and I had gone to Climb Iowa, the new climbing gym near Des Moines. I hadn't thought to invite Mom to go with us. I wasn't much of a gym climber anyway. I just thought it would be something for Chad and me to do during the snowy winter weeks.

I smiled, imagining Mom sitting at her computer in the kitchen at my parents' house, clicking around on the Climb Iowa website, finding the page about its classes, and then telling Kathy Stubbs at work about it.

She was sixty now, going climbing. I remembered her being one of the more protective mothers in my circle of friends. Never overbearing, just cautious. And now she was going to the climbing gym to learn how to belay.

"I think your mother's getting more adventurous as she gets older," my dad said when I asked him about it.

I laughed.

⸺

As my number of sober days stacked up into the thousands, I started to have less and less patience for drunk people.

I liked to be safe at home on weekend nights before people got too out of control in the city, and I hardly ever found myself in a bar anymore; I think my friends didn't see the point in taking me to a bar if they were going to be the only one drinking. But every once in a while, I'd run into someone who'd had a little too much. When you're sober, seeing that can feel like defusing a mildly dangerous, unpredictable bomb that reminds you of yourself a long time ago.

One night, Nick and I met up for a plate of nachos at the Irish Snug, a usually very low-key bar on Colfax. We grabbed two barstools and sat down, me scanning the bottles behind the bar and mentally checking off the taste of each one I'd drunk. I ordered a water.

The guy sitting on my other side was just looking for a little conversation, but I was hoping he'd eventually stop talking to us and walk away.

I'm too nice on the outside, sir, to tell you that I just came in here to get some food with my buddy and talk about life and catch up, and we actually don't need you to lean into our conversation and my arm as you knock back your ninth beer or whatever it is.

At first it was just annoying, but eventually I was starting to get mad enough that I was calculating which way to shove him so he wouldn't land on a table full of people.

And then, just like that, he said he had to go to the bathroom, and he shuffled off and didn't come back.

Take it easy, tough guy, I said to myself as Nick talked and I got back to listening.

Every once in a while, I get this feeling that I'm missing out, and that it's somehow unfair. I know it's pathetic that after all these years I would feel cheated because I can't drink. I know that billions of people don't drink and they don't care.

But there's everyone else. At five o'clock, they can take a load off and have a beer. Hell, maybe five. They can go ahead and pour a hot bath and a glass of cabernet, get a snifter of cognac with a cigar.

It's been a long day, they can say. *Why not grab the sports section and an ice-cold one. Throw some steaks on the grill and toss back a couple while cooking dinner. Go to that place that always has the live music and get a gin and tonic with the good gin. Let's toast life/love/women/our friendship/dead authors/ the greatest living quarterback. It's been a long week, right?*

Man, you know what's been a long time? Since I relaxed like that. I don't know how to explain to people that I get tired of walking this exact straight line and never deviating in the slightest.

I realize that I could have been born with no legs or diagnosed with terminal cancer and that an addiction problem isn't really too bad of a hand to be dealt in life. I remind myself of this when I get angry or feel sorry for myself.

⸺

I still find myself out at two or three in the morning every once in a while. I see all the partiers as I drive my Subaru past the bars in Denver's Capitol Hill neighborhood on my way to the freeway, but I'm on the other side of my day—the end of their Saturday was the beginning of my Sunday. A big day in the mountains requires an extra-early start, and I sip coffee in my car as people mill around outside bars and stagger to or from parties.

One of those 2 a.m. alarms for a 4:30 a.m. start was Quandary Peak near Breckenridge. I'd thought it was a great idea to climb up a snow couloir to fourteen thousand feet and then ski down. But it meant another bout of altitude sickness.

I knew it was coming. I kicked my crampons into the steep snow, noticing the low hum of dull pain at the base of my skull. My ski boots were just barely small enough to squeeze into my crampons. Chris and Nick were behind, following in my footsteps, poking through the snow to the rocks underneath. The three of us slowly made our way up the north couloir, our skis A-framed on our backpacks and our ice axes in hand.

Generally, when I was above twelve thousand feet, I was pretty miserable. It always started with a headache, and I knew I had just a few hours before I'd need to descend. The only thing that changed every time I went up high in the mountains was what else happened. Sometimes it became a full-blown migraine, with nausea plus lethargy, and I ended up walking with my mouth hanging open. Sometimes I had to make an emergency bathroom stop in a very uncomfortable place—a rock gully, as far as I could run from a campsite in the middle of the night and dig a hole, wherever.

Chris and Nick were fine, as all my friends usually are. I don't know what's different about me, what makes me so susceptible to altitude sickness. Every time, I tried to remember what I'd done that morning and the day before, and swore to do something different the next time: Hydrate more the day before. Don't drink a second cup of coffee the morning of the climb. Eat more. Drink more water. Maybe take a CamelBak so I could sip water all day instead of gulping it out of bottles whenever we stopped, which was apparently not often enough.

Near the top of the couloir, I started to lose my appetite, despite having just climbed two thousand feet of snow. Chris took the lead as the snow started to disintegrate. The inch of quickly melting white on top of the talus made our ice axes useless. We popped out of the top of the couloir and looked west.

"It's still so far," Nick said, sounding crestfallen, as Chris bolted off to the top.

"Nah, it's only a little bit more walking," I said. "You'll be fine."

I did not feel fine. I just wanted to get to the top so we could get down.

"You know, I don't even need to go to the summit," Nick said. "I can just meet you guys on your way down."

"Come on," I said. "You went through all that to almost go to the top?" It was only a few hundred feet of low-angle walking on a crust of snow.

"Have you done this?" he said, now lying facedown with his cheek on the snow, arms at his sides, backpack and skis on top of him. "It feels so good."

"Let's go," I said. "You can do it." I trudged slowly in Chris's footprints.

Nick moved his arms to push himself up off the snow, and I knew he would follow me. Nick had survived exactly a decade of our friendship as of this month, and this is what it had gotten him, poor guy. "Let's try rock climbing," I'd say," "Or mountain climbing. Or backcountry skiing." And he would be game.

The key difference was that I always wanted to summit, to reach the goal, no matter how meaningless it really was in the grand scheme of things. He couldn't give a shit either way. I'd seen it many times, most notably on Devils Tower the previous summer. We'd run out of water and had a typical beginner epic on the *Durrance Route*. But he got to the summit of Devils Tower, I told myself. Maybe in some way, it was a good memory for him.

I think he always came along because we were good friends with similar pain tolerances, and it seemed more interesting than sitting and talking at a café table in Denver all weekend.

He typically forgot to bring a camera to every single beautiful place we ever went. "Where's your camera?" I'd ask. "One of these days, I'm gonna make you a coffee-table book called *Photos of Nick Bohnenkamp in Beautiful Places* so you can fucking remember all these great trips we've been on." And then I did, with forty-five dollars and eight hours of my time, for his thirtieth birthday.

Chris was waiting at the summit when Nick and I slogged over the final bump. We took a quick self-portrait and started to descend. Chris clicked into his skis right on the summit and took off, and Nick and I walked a little ways down before putting ours on. It was tough to make turns in the late spring snow, pushing my ski edge hard into slush one moment, then punching through crust the next and bending my ski pole as I fell on it. My headache pounded even worse with the strain.

At the base of the steep part of the east face, I skied out to the ridge to wait for Nick. I clicked out of my skis and sat down on a rock, waiting to vomit. *No Nick on the slope, not even at the top. Where is he?* I hoped he was okay. There was no way I was going to be able to climb up and find him.

A couple, in shorts and jackets, hiked down the melted-out rock path on the far south edge of the east face, where the summer trail was. Finally, behind them, I saw Nick. He was walking, slowly, and carrying his skis over his shoulder. The couple hustled down the ridge, leaving Nick behind as he crept down. He had taught himself to snowboard during his first season as a ski bum/lift operator at Breckenridge six years before but hadn't quite figured out skis. I was decent, maybe a little below average for Coloradoans, with just enough knowledge to survive easier backcountry ski terrain in variable conditions.

I looked along the ridge below me. No one was coming up. I imagined Chris sitting on a rock in the sun down there, eating a sandwich and wondering about Nick and me. I closed my eyes, put my head in my hands, and pushed on my cheekbones, trying to relocate some of the pressure and mitigate my altitude sickness. I belched for the fiftieth time in the past three hours, wondering if I'd even be hungry for dinner when we got back.

Altitude sickness was a nagging, recurring issue, a little reminder from the mountains saying, *Hey, Iowa kid, you only* think *you're a mountain climber.* Maybe I had problems with my lungs because of all the cigarettes I'd smoked before I finally quit three and a half years earlier. Sometimes I felt like I should just find a new, lower-altitude hobby. But I wanted to be in those mountains so bad, bad enough to put up with altitude sickness a few times a year, I guess.

The hiking couple reached my rock when Nick was still a tiny figure way up there on the ridge, working hard to not fall over in the wind, his skis becoming something of a sail. I said hello as they passed me. As soon as they were out of sight, I cleared out a hole in the talus behind the rock, pulled my pants down and relieved my altitude-induced digestion. If anyone else came up the trail and saw me, I was too sick to be embarrassed, or care.

Ten minutes later, Nick walked up and announced that walking down the ridge with his skis was the single most terrifying thing he'd ever done. I figured in a couple of weeks it would seem less terrifying.

Skiing a fourteen-thousand-foot peak was a funny thing, I guess, for a couple of guys who met waiting tables at an Applebee's in Iowa. We weren't necessarily good at it, but I was proud we actually survived all the things we'd done together.

⸻

I went back to Quandary two and a half months later, this time with my mom. We had hatched a plan to get her up her first fourteener for her birthday. She was fit, I figured, and no matter how slowly we climbed up in the thin air, I knew she wouldn't quit. We picked a Friday in September to try, and got a good weather forecast.

It was dark outside the Safeway in Breckenridge at 6 a.m. as Mom and I walked around the aisles, looking at the potato chip bags swelled taut with the altitude.

"You have to eat breakfast before we start hiking, Mom," I had told her several times. "We're going to burn through hundreds of calories in a couple hours, and you don't want to run out of energy. I can bring you a fruit smoothie to drink in the car when I pick you up at 4 a.m., or whatever you want."

"I'm just not hungry right when I wake up," she'd told me for the tenth time, and I finally gave up. Now, at Safeway, she poked around the donut case as I tried to look patient, but I worried that we wouldn't be on the summit before noon and on our way down before the afternoon thunderstorms rolled in.

"I think I'm going to buy one of those inflatable pumpkins for Mary," she said. "Do you want one?" My niece, Chad and Meg's first child, was well on her way to having fifty stuffed animals in her room. I had contributed to that. But an inflatable pumpkin? Whatever.

"Nah, I'm good. Thanks, though," I said.

I'd tried to plan for everything on Quandary Peak, explain everything to my mom. It wasn't a big deal for me, but for my mother it was, enough so for me to worry about it. And she was going to launch her summit bid on her first fourteener fueled by a nutritious breakfast of a single fucking donut.

⸺

A mile into the hike, as the sun lit the upper part of the east face and we popped out of the forest, Mom slipped on a rock step, bashing her shin. "You okay, Mom?" I asked.

"I think so," she said.

When I looked closer, I saw dark blood running out of her skin right over the shinbone, a slowly growing drip. *How does your worrying about your parents when they start to get older compare to how much they worried about you when you were a kid?*

I stopped and pulled out my first-aid kit, which consisted of a tube of Krazy Glue and two feet of duct tape in a small roll. We washed off her leg and wiped the blood off with a tissue from the pocket of her fleece jacket.

"I always carry this, but I've never used it," I said, holding up the Krazy Glue. "Is it safe?"

"I think so," she said. "I'm sure it's similar to Dermabond or medical glue."

"I'm gonna let you do it, then," I said, deferring to Mom's medical degree and decades of experience as a nurse and nurse practitioner.

After that, she charged up the trail just behind me, a little lady in white running shoes. I reminded her too often to drink water and eat, because we were at high altitude.

We cranked out the three thousand feet of elevation gain, slowing a little bit near the top, and sat down on the summit in the sun to have a snack and stare at the repeating ridges of high peaks to the east and west. I pulled out two cans of Starbucks Doubleshot and took a photo of us clinking the cans together, then asked another hiker to take a photo of Mom and me, on top of the biggest hill we'd ever climbed.

When I arrived back at my parents' house the next Christmas, Mom had both photos in a frame on the bookshelf.

IDENTITY

MY FRIEND MICK AND I had just jumped the safety railing at Point Imperial on the North Rim of the Grand Canyon. We were starting the approach to Mount Hayden, a three-hundred-foot spire popping up into the air above the deep pit of the most famous canyon in the world. Tourists who stand at Point Imperial with a telephoto lens can get a shot of climbers standing on Mount Hayden's tabletop summit three-quarters of a mile away. That is, if they get lucky enough to see one of the fifty or so people who top out on it every year. Mick, twenty years my senior but tougher and fitter, had taken nine days off work from his tree service business to go on a desert road trip with me. Mick had climbed hundreds of trees to trim branches but hadn't climbed much rock and wasn't familiar with the systems for something like this. He was always up for an adventure, though. This was the one day on the trip I was nervous about.

We had ten and a half hours of daylight to descend to the saddle between the North Rim and the base of Mount Hayden, then hike to the start of the route. We would tackle three hundred feet of roped climbing on questionable sandstone to the summit, complete three rappels down, and hike back up to Point Imperial.

New Mexico locust trees, which sport sturdy thorns a half inch to an inch long down the length of every one of their branches, were packed into our route to the saddle as tight as the people in the first ten rows at a concert. There was no trail, so we aimed ourselves into what was little more than controlled falling down the steep slope of loose dirt, weaving between the trees all the way, wanting nothing more than to be able to grab a tree for support. The thorns didn't care that we were trying to avoid them, jabbing through our leather work gloves and double-front Carhartt pants.

At the end of the gully, we bushwhacked sideways across the slope through more thorns, losing the advantage of gravity. Then we crossed the saddle, moving over almost untouched shattered-red-sandstone gravel toward the tower. We headed around to the south face, where we were invisible to anyone who might be at the Point Imperial viewpoint. The only sign of other humans were the tour helicopters that flew past to the southeast, hovering above the Colorado River.

I reviewed belay techniques with Mick, who had climbed with me a few times before. I cursed myself for not taking him out for a couple less committed climbing days before this trip. I wanted to climb Mount Hayden without worrying if his belay would catch me if I fell. Too late for that.

Two pitches went by quickly, challenging climbing but not scary, at least for me. Mick followed with the backpack, carefully but naturally moving up the sandstone. I worked my way to the base of a chimney at the start of the third pitch and looked up into it. And that was when I got nervous.

I couldn't see many holds on either side, and I could tell I'd have to use opposing pressure to get up it—one foot on one side, one foot on the other, or feet pushing on one side, back pushing against the other. I couldn't talk myself into going up it or convince myself that Mick could follow me up it with a backpack on his back, so I climbed to the left, creating a tremendous amount of tension as the rope zigzagged between carabiners clipped to the cams lining the cracks below me.

I knew I was off route, climbing across bushes, breaking off pieces of rock in my hands, hoping footholds wouldn't explode under my feet. I stopped to anchor myself in and bring Mick up, pulling the rope through my horrendously wandering route. The friction between all the carabiners made it feel like my rope was tied to the bumper of a car that I was trying to haul up the face. Finally, I ran out of rope, and Mick began to climb.

Next pitch, I continued off-route, after pulling my way up a difficult hand crack. I wandered all over the south face of the tower, trying to find a route to the summit that I could both confidently climb and Mick could follow. *What an amateur I am.*

I took deep breaths, trying to calm myself down. We didn't have much daylight, and my poor navigation was costing us precious minutes. And I kept thinking of things that could go wrong: *What if I broke a hold and it fell and hit Mick, knocking him out?* We were close to the rim of the canyon, but we were on the south face of the rock, the side pointing toward the Colorado River and the South Rim. You'd need a telescope to see us from the South Rim. No one knew where we were, besides Mick's wife, back in Colorado, who might not know who to call if we didn't call her from the Winnebago tonight and tell her we had made it out okay.

I should have stayed home. What the hell am I doing out here? Looking for "adventure?" Maybe not the best place to bring your inexperienced friend. If things start to go wrong right now, this could turn into the real deal. The canyon below us is going to turn into a big cold hole, and if we don't want to spend the night in it, we have to get onto the rim before dark.

Fortunately, I found a way, and got us back onto the real route. After too many hours of climbing, I sat in the autumn sun on the tabletop summit of Mount Hayden. Popping my climbing shoes off, I pulled in rope as

Mick followed me up. It felt like we were on top of a clock tower in the middle of a city of red and brown ridges and buttes. I was blown away by where I stood, though in the back of my mind I was thinking, *We still have to rappel off this thing and battle back up that horrible slope of thorns.*

⸺

We had three rappels, and each one consumed way too much time, because the ropes got tangled, stuck in bushes and cracks. I had to slide myself down the rope, carefully slowing just before a giant knot, then pull up rope to untangle it. *Too much time, too much time.*

The sun was creeping down to the west, and the canyon below us grew darker and darker. Every rappel, I threw the ropes and watched them twist themselves into a mess as they fell halfway down. My heart sank.

We hit solid ground at the bottom of the last rappel with a little more than an hour to make it back up to the rim before sunset. It had taken us two hours to get *down* the same distance.

We hacked our way across the slope of New Mexico locust, my mind jogging back to the gauntlet drill in my high school football practices, where six teammates would form two lines and I would run between them with the ball as they all swatted at me, trying to knock the ball loose. Instead of twelve arms, I now rushed through dozens of tree branches that felt like they were armed with nails. I was too tired to be careful, and the thorns tore at my shirt, pants, hands. I kept my sunglasses on through the dying light to protect my eyes. I swatted at trees, I lunged. Once I lunged too hard and fell forward into another mess of thorny branches, frustrated, ready to kick and scream and throw a fit like a spoiled child.

We tripped up the slope, keeping our eyes on a tall ponderosa pine we knew was next to the viewpoint. It was dark by this point. I left my headlamp off, wanting to be able to see the distant rim instead of what was directly in front of my feet. I trudged upward on autopilot. Mick was ahead of me, moving silently.

At last, I grabbed the handrail at Point Imperial and pulled myself over. I dropped my pack on the sidewalk and sat down on the steps.

I don't know what keeps you going in those situations in the wilderness, when all you want is to sit down and stop, give up on getting home, let it get dark, and fall asleep on the side of a trail or against a rock. But you don't—you keep pushing, putting one foot in front of the other, numb to the heavy pack full of ropes and gear on your back. Sometimes it's adrenaline, maybe that last handful of M&M's, or some other brain process that connects the desire to get home to your friends and family again to the muscles that move your legs.

At the end, when you get to the car, or the tent, or just the bottom of the climb, your brain finally understands, *I am not going to die today.* There is no more doubt, no more fear, and you are warmed with a feeling of satisfaction, just enough that you start thinking, *Hey, maybe I'd do that again. Not anytime soon, but what a day.*

Coming down from those days, you enjoy a comparatively easy life. Instead of fretting about stuck rappel ropes, or handholds breaking, or twenty-foot whippers into the side of the rock, you stand happily in the grocery store trying to decide between black beans or refried for the burritos you're going to cook at the campground that night. And that's fun. You smile. It's enjoyable, to come back to the safer, grounded world that you dreamed about escaping, and realizing that even if you burn your burritos, it's a tiny worry compared to wondering if you're going to get yourself and your buddy killed on some stupid rock in a canyon in Arizona.

The next night, Mick and I sat at the dining table of his twenty-year-old Winnebago Warrior at the Watchman Campground in Zion National Park. We didn't have a chance to stop at a store on our way there, and Mick was out of beer. I didn't think much of it at the time, since he only had four or five microbrews each night. But after dinner, we hardly spoke a word. I tried to engage him and got short answers, or one-word replies. Our usually limitless flow of conversation—on women, on life, on midlife crises, on climbing, on travel, on political issues and religious differences—had dried up. He'd been reading the newspaper for two hours, and there couldn't have been more than thirty minutes of material.

I glanced around the camper, trying to make conversation every few minutes, wondering if it was the lack of beer that made Mick so quiet. Did I used to feel the same way he did, when I didn't have a couple of drinks in me? My fun friend, the engaging conversationalist, the guy who never ran out of stories, he was gone for the night. His engine sputtered and died after it ran out of fuel. Was he just tired? It seemed like too much of a coincidence that the one night he was sullen the whole trip was the night there was no beer in the fridge.

⌐⌐

Over the next three years, Mick and I would talk on and off about his drinking. To me, it hadn't seemed like much, but I often remembered that night in the camper, how it seemed like something was missing. I told him maybe it would be a good idea to quit completely. He disagreed, saying he thought he could do it in moderation. It was a conversation I'd heard in my own head at age twenty-three, and one that I continued to have: *I can control it. No, you can't. Yes, I can. No, you can't.* At one point, Mick and I even argued. We let it get between us, and didn't get together as often as we should have. Eventually, we both apologized, and things returned to normal.

He quit drinking six weeks before he died. Things were going really well, his wife told me. Then one day, his heart just stopped. He was fifty-four. At the funeral, Mick's son, Dan, mentioned our Mount Hayden climb in his eulogy. Not a week went by without his voice popping into my head.

⌐⌐

As the radius of my travels around the West extended farther from my roots, Iowa became less of a familiar place. Wedding invitations tapered off, and my parents moved two hours away from my hometown. When I went to visit them, I wouldn't run into any high school classmates at the grocery store. The month after Mick died, I went back for Christmas, to spend time with Mom and Dad, Chad and Meg—and Grandma, who was gradually slowing down.

"Is this another goddamn fruitcake?" she asked me on Christmas morning, holding the gift-wrapped box. When you're an eighty-two-year-old lady, using profanity is endearing. She was sitting in her bathrobe at the end of the couch next to a cup of coffee with a teaspoon of sugar stirred into it. It was clear I was going to have to get creative about wrapping to fool her next year.

Two Christmases prior, I had found out how much Grandma hated fruitcake, so I'd grabbed one at the grocery store before my flight from Denver and wrapped it up, giving it to her on Christmas morning after she'd opened her other gifts from me, which always included two pounds of good coffee beans.

"No, no, it's not," I said now. "Just open it." Grandma and I had become very good buddies over hundreds of cups of coffee and cookies. When she visited, I slept in the basement so she could have a decent bed, and I always helped her in and out of the car. Out of her seven children, she visited us the most, at least partly because Mom, her oldest child, would never let her sit alone in her big empty house in Emmetsburg for very long. When Grandma stopped being able to drive the two and a half hours to Mom and Dad's house, Mom drove to pick her up. Like I said, in my family, love is attendance-based.

"It *is* a fruitcake, you jerk." Grandma laughed, and I laughed, and I took a photo of her holding it. Just like the year before, we sat it on the kitchen table for an hour or so before throwing it in the trash. Every year for five years, I bought her a fruitcake and we did the exact same thing.

Mom started to remind me before every visit back to Iowa, "Don't forget your climbing harness and shoes." She had kept going to the climbing gym, and when I arrived, the second or third thing she'd ask me would be, "What day do you want to go climbing?"

I watched Mom put on her climbing harness at one of the picnic tables at Climb Iowa, the thirty-foot-high walls behind her speckled with a rainbow of plastic holds, strung with ropes and autobelays every five feet. I noticed one of the leg loops was upside down, something I've caught myself doing half a dozen times. I reached over and flipped it over for her.

After she climbed a route, I tied into the end of the rope, inspected Mom's belay device to make sure the rope ran through it correctly to arrest a fall, chalked up my hands, and climbed up the first twelve feet. I looked down at my waist and noticed a couple feet of slack in the rope. Mom wasn't keeping up. Hanging from two good handholds, I turned around and looked down at her. She was working hard to try to keep taking in slack and keep the belay locked off at the same time, but she wasn't fast enough. If I climbed up thirty feet and took a fall, she might have ten feet of slack in the rope. When it caught me, it would snap taut and hurt, maybe injure me.

"You okay, Mom?" I asked.

"I think so," she said, furiously pulling short bits of rope through the belay device, struggling.

"I'm going to climb down and see if I can help you do that a little more efficiently." I started back down.

"Okay, Mom," I said, on the floor, watching her. "You want to pull on the rope that's coming out of your belay device and going up to the anchor up there, pull on that toward you as you pull rope out of the belay device with your other hand. Try to get more rope in each pull so you're not doing it a hundred times in a minute. Let's practice that a few times, and then I'll get back on the route and climb slowly."

I took my time, looking down every other move to see Mom keeping up better. She would need a little more practice before I could start climbing full-speed without worrying. We were both slow learners, I think, especially with physical skills. Which is probably why I only know how to tie five knots—the minimum I needed to do the climbs I did.

An hour later, I started up an overhanging toprope route on the far right side of the gym, already a little tired. Two-thirds of the way up the wall, my forearms were pumped. I looked down to see Mom doing great, almost underneath me, because the wall overhung by eight or ten feet. My heart pounded, and my arms burned. *Two more moves until the wall goes back vertical. I can do it. I can't do it. I can do it.* I lurched for one more hold, hoping I could freeze my fingers in a claw and hang on. *Nailed it.*

Nope.

I'm fucked. No way I can hold on. My hands started to open, and a sixty-year-old 110-pound woman who had been climbing maybe five times in her life hung on to the end of the rope as I whipped off the wall twenty feet above her head. I fell through the open space under the fluorescent lights, swung out from the wall, and stopped midair. She caught me.

Nice job, Mom. I was glad it was a toprope, distributing the force of my fall through the anchor at the ceiling so she wouldn't have to catch the full force of a lead fall, which would have yanked her off her feet and into the air.

"I think I'm done," I yelled down.

"You sure?" Mom yelled back up.

"Yeah, I think that's good for today. Let's go get milk shakes."

She lowered me down to the carpet. We popped off our climbing shoes and harnesses and packed up. Mom went into the bathroom, and I milled around the lobby waiting for her. One of the guys on the staff came over.

"Was that your mom climbing with you?" he asked.

"Yep," I said. "We come in here every time I visit. I'm trying to get her up some 5.7s now."

"That's so cool that she knows how to belay and everything," he said.

"We have a lot of fun. She loved the class she took here with her friend." I looked out through the glass into the gym, calm on a weekday afternoon. A man was belaying a woman leading a route. The only other climbers were young kids, whose mothers sat on the benches as their seven- and eight-year-olds scampered up the walls, clipped into the autobelay ropes. When they came down, the moms would get up and unclip them, then clip them into another rope and sit back down. Mom was definitely the only climbing grandmother there. She was unique. I smiled.

Mom liked climbing—the challenge, the exercise, and relating to me. We worked together. I taught her things I had learned in my hundreds of pitches of climbing: keep your weight on your feet, drop your knee, look at the route as a series of moves between rests. I think it gave her a better idea of what I did back in Colorado.

⸺

As life became a little more serious and busy, with more responsibility at my job, I climbed not out of the beginner's fervor, but to center myself. I appreciated the relaxation that came with concentrating on nothing but moving through a route without falling, pushing all my other concerns into the background.

I'd left the newspaper for a nonprofit job, running a fund-raiser for Big City Mountaineers, an organization that took at-risk urban youth on wilderness trips. I kept writing and trying to get published, sending out article pitches after work and getting a few stories published in the *Mountain Gazette*, on *The Dirtbag Diaries* podcast, and in a few other small publications. But lately, the office had taken over my sanity: We'd had three executive directors in less than a year, and my boss was about to leave for a different job, giving me full responsibility of a program that used to be run by three employees.

Meridian Hill was Lee's idea. "Meridian Hill, Meridian Hill," he'd been saying to me for two years. "Unclimbed. No one there. First ascents for the taking. If this rock was in Boulder Canyon, people would be all over it," Lee said.

Unfortunately for us, it wasn't in Boulder Canyon, where the longest approach hike to any rock climb is about forty-five minutes, and most are fifteen to twenty minutes. Meridian Hill is in the Mount Evans Wilderness, an hour's drive from Denver, and a two-hour cross-country hike from a dirt road. I took a day off work for it, telling myself it was for mental health.

We parked the truck at 8 a.m. and hiked in. Lee led a fun first pitch up good rock, stopping at a ledge to belay. My lead. I padded up some easy moves to the base of a crack I thought would be good, but it turned out to be less than an inch deep. I tried to stuff my fingers in, hoping for some kind of invisible feature in the seam that could function as a handhold. From forty feet below, it had looked like a good line to climb up. On it, I found that it had about as many handholds as someone's living room wall. Shit. I stepped right, hoping the next seam over was better. If I lost my balance, I'd skid down about twenty feet and probably swing over underneath Lee, belaying me from a ledge a hundred feet off the ground.

Well, at least this trip to Lee's "secret crag" ought to get him to stop bugging me about it, I thought. It was scary to climb, and insecure. The rock was good, but it was missing cracks to place protective gear. Still, Lee was right—the whole place was practically untouched by climbers. It was exciting to climb a legitimate two-hundred-foot route that was an open canvas. Wherever I said the route goes, it goes. And right now, I hoped it would go up this seam.

I smeared my shoes across the granite and plugged a cam in halfway, wondering if it would even hold me if I fell. Fifty feet of climbing later, I worked my way onto a ledge, and the angle of the rock backed off. It was the end of the route. My new route. My first-ever "first ascent."

It was exactly what I needed, Meridian Hill, climbing untouched granite in the sunshine, even if it was on one-star routes that no one would ever repeat. It was the last day of September, and work had been insanity. I hadn't been sleeping well at night, sometimes waking up to respond to an email or make myself a to-do list.

That morning when I'd met Lee to drive to the crag, I had forgotten my belt and my socks. As I plugged in gear to build an anchor so Lee could climb up to me now, I checked the shoelace running through my belt loops to make sure it was still tied.

A slight breeze blew on my face, and sitting on a ledge of granite that has likely never seen a human foot or hand, I leaned back and watched a golden eagle hang in a thermal, just sitting in the air, wings out. I rested my helmet against the rock and took in rope as Lee started to climb up, one hundred feet below, out of view under the bulge of the rock beneath me.

The words "This is what I do" rolled into my head as I watched the bird. I climb. That's what I do.

I work at a nonprofit, and I'm a writer and a brother and an uncle and a son. But this is what I love, what inspires me. I am relaxed for the first time in weeks because I am out here on this ledge, finding a line up a granite wall and following my instincts.

I am a climber, finally identified by something I do instead of something I don't do.

FOREVER

I WATCHED GRANDMA PICK AT THE Maid-Rite sandwich from the shop down the street. She was only interested in the chocolate milk shake. I'd flown from Denver to Des Moines and rented a car on the spur of the moment. I felt like I had to do something, even if I just sat in the room and talked to her.

A few days before, my mom had told me over the phone that Grandma was in the hospital, again, with an infection. She'd gotten a fever while staying with Mom and Dad. She was confused and had lots of swelling.

"Mom, do you think I should come?" I'd asked.

"Oh, I don't know," she'd said. "It's probably expensive, and you're busy."

"I'll get a flight for Tuesday," I'd said.

I had left my nonprofit job and had slowly collected enough freelance writing gigs that I could write full-time. I'd finally gotten bylines in a few national magazines, including *Climbing*, where I was now a contributing editor. In a month, I was flying to Norway with Forest, a photographer, and my old climbing buddy Chris, to explore a little-known granite climbing area.

The freedom of self-employment meant I could work from anywhere, and I'd been living out of my van for almost two years, traveling, climbing, exploring, and writing stories and a blog from coffee shops and public libraries. I loved the idea of being a vagabond writer, even if it was frustratingly inconvenient at times. The freedom of making my own schedule meant I could go anywhere whenever I wanted—including a spur-of-the-moment trip home to visit my grandmother in the hospital.

Every time Grandma got sick, Mom ran herself ragged going back and forth across the elevated walkway from the medical clinic where she worked to Grandma's hospital room. She checked on her in the morning, then at noon during the lunch break she never took anyway, then after she left the office, late every day.

This time, my uncle Dan drove an hour from Perry, where he ran a dental practice, to check in. We caught up while he joked with Grandma.

"Mom, we're so optimistic we're gonna buy you some green bananas," he said, and we laughed.

I sat with Grandma for three days, arriving in the morning, leaving in the afternoon when she took a nap, and coming back again around dinner to stay in the room with Mom until Grandma went to sleep for the night. Mom wanted me to try to talk Grandma into moving into an assisted living home. Grandma was forgetting things, leaving food in the oven for hours. A handyman had come to fix her clothes dryer and found the vent clogged with feet of packed lint.

I was supposed to help convince her that it was okay to leave her house. On paper it was the best solution: close to Mom and Dad, easy for her other kids in Iowa, and close to an airport so my aunts living in Florida, Ohio, and Oregon could visit. Things would be taken care of for her.

I tried, but my heart wasn't in it.

"Brendan," she said, "can you imagine me living in a tiny little apartment, giving up my house? I don't want to go somewhere I don't know anyone."

I couldn't imagine it. The house was all she had left of her independence, and her sense of identity.

———

Every time I walked out of the automatic hospital doors, I sat in my little red rental car and let tears stream down my face. My brother couldn't get time off work to get here on such short notice, but if he were here, he would not be out here crying like a fucking baby. I was supposed to be planning a climbing trip in Norway in four weeks, figuring out how we'd come back with a story for the magazine—not losing my shit twice a day in the parking lot of a hospital in Iowa. It was easier when I kept my distance, just stayed in Denver and got updates from my mom. It hurt less.

We went up and down the hospital hallways, following doctor's orders, Grandma pushing a walker and taking five-inch steps forward while I rolled the IV bag next to her. We probably covered eighty feet in ten minutes, and she apologized over and over again for being so slow.

"Grandma, I'm not in a hurry," I told her. "I don't have anywhere else to be."

"I bet you can walk anywhere you want."

"Yeah, Grandma," I said. "I guess I can."

I thought about all the places I had walked, like the top of the Grand Teton and the bottom of the Grand Canyon. I don't know why she had to say something like that shuffling along in a hospital gown. I don't know why it made me so sad.

Three days later, I loaded Grandma into my rental car and drove her to Mom and Dad's. I took a photo of us in the car, both of us giving the camera a thumbs-up, and texted it to all her kids.

A few weeks later, I flew to Norway and climbed enormous slabs of granite, a swath of gray rock two and a half miles long and twenty-five hundred feet high, tucked away in a dead-end valley inhabited by ten people. I battled up the hardest finger crack of my life, and on Forest's birthday, we climbed a five-thousand-foot 5.4 to the top of a peak, and we slept on our ropes, piled on the rocks at the summit, and watched the sun set over the fjords as it dipped below the horizon for only four hours.

As I was flying across the ocean from Bergen to Denver, Mom and her six brothers and sisters were moving Grandma and a small selection of things that reminded her of home into Glenwood Place, a big white vinyl-sided building full of sweet little old ladies and men at the southwest edge of Marshalltown. That was the beginning of the end for the woman all of us drew strength from.

Two days after Christmas that year, we went to Climb Iowa for the day—Mom, Chad, Meg, and Mary, my then-six-year-old niece. It was becoming a Christmas tradition, climbing for a couple of hours until we were tired, then driving to the Drake Diner in Des Moines to eat ice cream. Some days Mary liked to climb a lot, and some days she liked it when I picked her up by her harness's belay loop and swung her around with one hand. I wondered how many more years I'd be strong enough to do it.

Mom tied in at the base of a 5.7 route, saying she felt a little queasy, but she'd try the route anyway. She climbed to the top, and I lowered her. But at the bottom, she vomited, catching most of it in her hand. I hurriedly untied her so she could run to the women's restroom. I found some paper towels and blotted up the small mess at the base of the climbing wall.

Five minutes later, she came back over, saying she felt better, and maybe it was just something she ate. She climbed a couple more routes and managed to down an ice-cream sundae at the diner.

As we drove back to Marshalltown, and I went with her to the pharmacy to pick up a prescription for Grandma, and Mom started shivering.

"You don't look so good, Mom," I said. "Why don't I drop you off at home so you can rest, and I'll go check on Grandma at her apartment and drop off the medicine?"

"I'm fine," she said, but I insisted she go home. I won, maybe for the first time in my life.

I texted Chad from the driveway: *Make sure Mom goes to bed.*

She didn't go to bed, instead sitting on the couch next to the Christmas tree with a blanket over her head, feeling like hell but not wanting to miss out on a minute of time with her grandkids—Mary and her little brother, Max.

I drove Mom's car to Grandma's tiny apartment and found her sitting on the couch, confused, with a 103.5 temperature. I hit the button for the attendant to help me out and texted Mom, *103.5.* She flew into action, off the couch next to the Christmas tree and down the street to Grandma's, pushing her own fever somewhere else for a few hours in an effort to rescue her own mother.

We began the slow epic of moving an eighty-six-year-old woman across icy sidewalks, into the car, and to the emergency room—me, Mom, and the attendant trying to gently get her to the passenger seat as she tried to get her feet to work, her brain cooking with fever.

"Just shuffle your right foot six inches, Grandma," I said. "Six inches. Okay, how about three?" In five minutes, we moved three feet.

At the ER entrance, we couldn't get her out of the car. "Grandma, grab my hands," I said, "I'll just pull you into the wheelchair." I pulled gently, and she didn't move. I felt like I was going to pull her arms off.

"Okay, Grandma," I said, "put your arms around my neck, and I'll give you a big bear hug."

I pulled, and she said, "I can't, I can't, I can't."

Mom ran inside the door and grabbed two paramedics, who lifted Grandma out in about thirty seconds, and we wheeled her inside, out of the icy night air.

Nobody in the emergency room was happy: the couple with the screaming kid, the other people waiting in the chairs for news about their loved one. You sit in the waiting room, just wanting everything to be better for the person you brought there, so you can all get back to normal life where all your loved ones are healthy.

I wheeled Grandma down the hall to room 11. Mom and I sat next to each other in two chairs next to the wall as nurses popped a blood pressure cuff on Grandma and plugged her into an IV. Mom mass-texted six brothers and sisters in four states.

I sat there and thought, *This Christmas is sad.*

"Why don't you call Dad and have him come pick you up," Mom said, looking up from her phone.

"Bullshit, Mom," I said. "You're the sick one. You need to go home."

"When I'm eighty-six, you can come sit by my hospital bed. I get this one."

I gave up, sent Dad a text message, and stepped outside the sliding doors to wait in the parking lot. I leaned up against the brick wall next to the ER entrance in the dark, wiping tears away with the sleeve of my puffy jacket.

━

In my van a couple of days later, with Grandma stable in the hospital and Mom feeling a little better, I asked Mom, "Do you think your brothers and sisters know how hard this is?"

"I don't think so," she said. "On Christmas they say things like 'We had a relaxing day'—and I think, 'I want to have a relaxing day. I worked all day!'"

"Mom, I think you're like me. I don't know if you've ever had a relaxing day in your life."

"No, *you're* like *me*," she said, emphatically. "I'm the mother."

We both laughed. I gently pressed the brake pedal so we wouldn't slide on the ice at a four-way stop. She pointed out a tree with multicolored big-bulb holiday lights, the only thing decorated in someone's spacious front yard at that intersection.

"I like that tree," she said. It was at the left turn to Mom and Dad's house. She'd made that left turn hundreds of times that year, driving home from Grandma's little apartment. Everybody else in the family, including me, got to drop in whenever our schedules allowed. But not Mom. She called every morning, at lunch, then left work late and stopped by to see Grandma every day. She drove past that tree with the big bulbs on it, got home at eight thirty, and went to bed about a half hour later every night.

———

In June I went back for a week, as the whole family did every year. Chad and Meg drove the kids over from Wisconsin, and I drove the twelve hours from Denver. Mom and Dad took the week off work, and we hung out in the humidity and went swimming and goofed around, and Max, age four, and now-seven-year-old Mary called my mom and dad Grandma Kathy and Papa Joe, and called me Uncle Brendan.

At the end of the week, Chad and Meg and the kids drove back to Wisconsin, and I flew to a friend's wedding in the shadow of Mount Rainier. The next time I went back, my aunt Nora had arrived from Florida to hang out with Grandma, cleaning her apartment and sleeping on the couch five feet away from her bed. I hung around Mom and Dad's for a couple of days, trying to ignore the itch to get back to Denver and get back to work.

I had a ton of work to do before I was supposed to meet Chris for a climbing trip in the Wind River Range in Wyoming, a trip I had felt increasingly hesitant about but couldn't figure out why. It would be an eight-hour drive to get there and an eight-hour drive to get back. I kept flipping through the Wind River guidebook and not finding the right combination of easy alpine climbs in an area that wasn't in the Cirque of the Towers, which would be crowded with other climbers.

———

On Monday evening, from the parking lot in front of Grandma's apartment, I called Chris, asking how he would feel about maybe doing something a little less committing. Maybe five days in Rocky Mountain National Park? It was close to Denver, so a little easier on me. I knew he loved the park. He said yes, and I felt a little relieved. I hung up and joined Mom and Aunt Nora for a walk with Grandma.

We rolled her around the man-made pond down the hill from her place. The park was one of those manicured bits of nature built into an expanding town, a few feet of hedgerow separating it from the cornfield behind, a busy street a hundred yards away across the water. The sun had dropped, sparing us the early June Iowa humidity—what Grandma always described as "muggy." I walked slowly behind the wheelchair, pushing her over a bridge that crossed the pond's outflow.

"Look at the birds," she said. They were the same ones we'd seen on our first lap, but she'd forgotten. She was a little confused, maybe already a little hypoxic. She didn't eat dinner that night and declined a cookie for perhaps the first time in seven decades.

⸻

The next morning, Mom knocked on my bedroom door, opening it a crack. "Grandma was unresponsive this morning when Nora tried to wake her up," she said. "I'm going to the ICU now."

I threw on some clothes, ate a rushed breakfast, and jumped in my van.

Grandma lay in bed, eyes closed and hooked to beeping machines, an oxygen mask strapped to her face as she tried to expel the carbon dioxide stuck in her lungs. A doctor talked to Mom and Aunt Nora, both nurses, and explained things in medical language they understood. There was a chance she would wake up and improve. Uncle Dan arrived, then Uncle Steve, my mom's tall brothers, two of my earliest heroes as a kid. Mom and Nora and I left to get some lunch.

Grandma battled all afternoon, waking up twice, opening her eyes and trying to form some words under the oxygen mask. Aunt Nora held her hand, wiped away Grandma's tears, and told her, "It's okay, Mom. We're all here."

I had told Mom the day before that I didn't think Grandma was having that much fun anymore, my way of saying maybe she's ready. But nobody was ready, including Grandma. The tears that came out of her eyes in those moments she woke up to see everyone around her still haunt me.

Her breathing became more erratic. I knew it couldn't go on long. I held her hand for the last half hour of her life, watching her heart rate drop on the monitor next to the bed—105, 92, 71, 52, 27, 0—tears rolling down my cheeks. The alarm on the breathing machine went off, going for seconds, then what felt like minutes. I wished someone would come in and shut it off, but after a few seconds, I just reached up and did it myself.

I let go of Grandma's hand and walked out of the hospital to call Chad. My voice cracked into the phone. "I think it was time. Grandma wasn't having fun. It was good she had all of us around her."

"Okay. Thanks for calling," he said. "How's Mom doing?" He sounded rock-solid. "We'll see you soon." His messy little brother hung up and melted down one more time in the hospital parking lot.

I got in my van and drove north out of town, looking for some Iowa gravel roads to make me feel better, like I used to do when I was sixteen. I turned down the first one on the right and watched the sun roll toward the horizon in my rearview mirror. I knew so many things I hadn't known when I was a teenager driving on these roads, and they did the exact same thing for me that they did back then: nothing, besides give me a place to go when I didn't want to go home.

There would be no more chances to ask Grandma about my grandfather, the Irish guy with the quirky sense of humor and the nebulous but often confirmed problem with alcohol.

Still, I didn't regret never asking Grandma about what was wrong with him, to verify the label I shared with him: alcoholic. I had been sober for a dozen years, and I had long ago rejected the idea that I could blame my mistakes on my family tree.

I didn't cry at Grandma's funeral, or at the cemetery.

⸺

I drove back to Colorado a few days after the funeral. Chris came to visit, and we drove to Estes Park. In five days, we climbed three multipitch routes at Lumpy Ridge and the north ridge of the Spearhead, high up in Glacier Gorge. But I never once felt right, not even at the start.

Heading up what I thought was the third pitch of Pear Buttress on our first day, I struggled to get my fingers into a tiny crack, desperately placing a cam around a corner and hoping it would hold, then falling, not at all surprised when it blew out. I was off route, off balance, climbing like shit, and scared more than ever of dying in the mountains.

Ten minutes after we finished the descent of the Spearhead, scrambling down the loose west face, a boulder ripped free. It sounded like a freight train as it tumbled, maybe where Chris and I had just been.

Two days later, we climbed Nun Buttress, the most perfect twin hand cracks I'd ever led, and I moved confidently, without quite feeling comfortable. At the top, we walked cross-country on the top of Deer Mountain, the early evening sun washing through the pine trees. I told Chris that maybe I don't like climbing so much for the climbing, but for that calm you feel when the dangerous part is over.

A month later, halfway around the world, in Switzerland, I stood on the bench out the back door of the Sasc Furä hut, looking up at the stars, after coming downstairs to use the bathroom in the middle of the night. Above me, even without my contact lenses, I knew what the black spot in the sky blocking the stars was: the immense north ridge of the Piz Badile.

We had given up on climbing it in the morning—the upper half of the three-thousand-foot route had iced up, and no one had summited in weeks. The trip had been kind of a flop. It was the rainiest summer the country had seen in fifty years, maybe even seventy. In four days, I'd managed only a day and a half of not-classic climbing, getting hardly any usable photos for my magazine assignment. But I wasn't ready to write off the trip entirely. Even though I had flown thousands of miles and might never return here, I had never gotten shut down in my entire climbing career. I figured I was due. And it was a hell of a place just to see.

I pulled up the hood on my jacket and put my hands in my pockets and thought, *I bet my dad would think this was pretty fucking wild. Rock climbing in Switzerland. Listening to bus-size swaths of rock rumble and rip off the sides of ten-thousand-foot peaks in the night, standing down here at this little hut with a fence of granite and glaciers separating me from Italy on the other side.* And it could have never happened. I'd been this close, really, to a way different life.

I've written letters to my parents in some incredible places, thinking about them as I watch the sun set on the Dolomites or listen to water drip off raft oars on the Colorado River at the bottom of the Grand Canyon or sit on top of a thousand-foot granite dome near the US-Mexico border, staring off into the desert as I pull in rope and have a few quiet moments before my climbing partner arrives.

The letters exist only in my head for a few seconds, and then they flit away as I come back to whatever I'm doing. But they're always the same, always something like this:

> Sorry about the times when you felt worried, humili-
> ated, disappointed, and sad about me, when I was getting
> arrested and crashing cars and intent on wrecking my life.
> Sorry you had to drop me off at jail and wonder if the
> whole town knew about me hitting rock bottom, and the
> group therapy nights, and the times when I let you down,
> and the other times when I made you worry if I was safe or
> even alive.

> If I had told you back then what would be on the other side
> of all that terrible stuff—the things I'm grateful to do now,
> that I can't believe happen sometimes, that I snap photos
> of so I won't forget them—I don't know if any of us would
> have believed it.

I never send the letters, or even write them down; I just send post-cards, and articles that my mom and dad read in magazines or on the internet. I call home every Sunday, and hope they know I'm happy.

Privately, I think about change, and how it's the hardest thing—the story we've been telling ourselves might not exactly be true. We lose a job, or get a life-changing diagnosis from a doctor, or someone comes home one day and tells us they don't love us anymore. We have to pick ourselves up off the floor and try to wrap our head around how to go on with life.

Plenty of recovering addicts who have stayed sober long enough will tell you, "If I hadn't quit, I'd be dead or in jail." The thing I realize, though, the longer and longer I stay sober, is that the bigger injustice would not be a life cut short, or a life inside a prison. It would be living the sadly ordinary life of a career alcoholic, sitting on a barstool and telling the same stories to the same half-friends for years and years, spending all that money on just enough drinks to get into a cozy haze every night.

Now, instead, most days, especially when I'm in the mountains, I feel good—not like something's missing.

If I hadn't quit drinking, yeah, maybe I'd be dead or in jail. But probably I'd just be missing out on an extraordinary life. And that would be a tragedy.

ACKNOWLEDGMENTS

First, thanks to my parents, Joe and Kathy, who didn't deserve the bullshit. They deserved a story with a happy ending. I hope this is it.

Thanks to Nick Bohnenkamp and Jayson Sime, my two closest friends, who have been there since the partying started, stayed through the hard times afterward, have never said no to a big day in the mountains, and have never been too busy to help move a couch into a new apartment.

Thanks to Hilary Oliver, who has edited everything I've written since we met, is my favorite adventure partner, and doesn't mind talking with me about big ideas in the grocery store instead of shopping efficiently and effectively.

Thanks to Fitz and Becca Cahall for always believing in my voice and believing in most of my story ideas, and for publishing the first version of this one, *The Dirtbag Diaries* podcast episode "Sixty Meters to Anywhere," in 2009.

Thanks to John Fayhee, who published the first story I ever wrote that ever mattered to me, "Alcoholism and Other Mountains I've Climbed," in the *Mountain Gazette* in 2006.

Thanks to my brother, Chad, for knowing I needed a climbing rope when I didn't know it.

Thanks to Judy Blunt, who was the first person to encourage me to write about the things that became the early beginnings of this book—jail and substance-abuse treatment—and workshop them in her creative nonfiction class at the University of Montana.

Thanks to Emily White, Kate Rogers, Laura Shauger, and everyone at Mountaineers Books who made this story come to life, as well as Kiele Raymond, who pushed me to write more after I thought the initial story was done.

Thanks to Lee Smith for teaching me to place trad gear and opening the door to so many long days in the mountains. Thanks to Chris

El-Deiry, Jack Sasser, Alan Stoughton, Teresa Bruffey, Brian Williams, and Tom Riley, who shared a rope with me during some of the most memorable moments of my climbing life. Thanks to Dustin Ewald for being the first person to convince me I might actually like climbing, and for taking the time to teach me.

ABOUT THE AUTHOR

HILARY OLIVER

BRENDAN LEONARD is the creator of Semi-Rad.com and a former contributing editor to *Climbing* magazine. His writing has appeared in *Alpinist*, *Outside*, *Backpacker*, *Adventure Journal*, *National Geographic Adventure*, and many other publications. He has cowritten and coproduced films that have won awards at the Banff Mountain Film and Book Festival and the 5Point Film Festival. He lives in Denver.

MOUNTAINEERS BOOKS is a leading publisher of mountaineering literature and guides—including our flagship title, *Mountaineering: The Freedom of the Hills*—as well as adventure narratives, natural history, and general outdoor recreation. Through our two imprints, Skipstone and Braided River, we also publish titles on sustainability and conservation. We are committed to supporting the environmental and educational goals of our organization by providing expert information on human-powered adventure, sustainable practices at home and on the trail, and preservation of wilderness.

The Mountaineers, founded in 1906, is a 501(c)(3) nonprofit outdoor recreation and conservation organization whose mission is "to enrich lives and communities by helping people explore, conserve, learn about, and enjoy the lands and waters of the Pacific Northwest and beyond." One of the largest such organizations in the United States, it sponsors classes and year-round outdoor activities throughout the Pacific Northwest, including climbing, hiking, backcountry skiing, snowshoeing, kayaking, camping, sailing, and more. The Mountaineers also supports its mission through its publishing division, Mountaineers Books, and promotes environmental education and citizen engagement. For more information, visit The Mountaineers Program Center, 7700 Sand Point Way NE, Seattle, WA 98115-3996; phone 206-521-6001; www.mountaineers.org; or email info@mountaineers.org.

Our publications are made possible through the generosity of donors and through sales of more than 600 titles on outdoor recreation, sustainable lifestyle, and conservation. To donate, purchase books, or learn more, visit us online:

MOUNTAINEERS BOOKS
1001 SW Klickitat Way, Suite 201 • Seattle, WA 98134
800-553-4453 • mbooks@mountaineersbooks.org • www.mountaineersbooks.org

OTHER TITLES YOU MIGHT ENJOY FROM MOUNTAINEERS BOOKS

Drawn
The Art of Ascent
Jeremy Collins
An intimate visual exploration of how to reconcile family, career, and personal passion, from one of the most influential artists in the world of climbing

Psychovertical
Andy Kirkpatrick
The story of what happens to a nice lower-class kid with dyslexia who gains control over his circumstances by clinging to giant stone faces, thousands of feet in the air, for days at a time

Cold Wars
Climbing the Fine Line between Risk and Reality
Andy Kirkpatrick
The sequel to *Psychovertical*, written with Kirkpatrick's trademark wit and honesty

Rowing into the Son
Four Young Men Crossing the North Atlantic
Jordan Hanssen
An account of the struggle of the only American team to compete in the first ocean-rowing race from New York to England

High Infatuation
A Climber's Guide to Love and Gravity
Steph Davis
Vivid, personal essays and prose poems about life, love, friendship, empowerment, and more told through a career in climbing